WILLIAM STILL

DYING TO LIVE

CHRISTIAN FOCUS PUBLICATIONS

Published by
Christian Focus Publications Ltd
Geanies House, Fearn IV20 1TW
Ross-shire, Scotland, UK.

Sheana Brown

Proof Reading Editing

ISBN 0 906 731 97 6

Cover illustration
by

Cover design
by
Seoris McGillivray

Printed & bound in Great Britain by
Cox & Wyman Ltd, Reading.

CONTENTS

INTRODUCTION

At various times in my ministry in Gilcomston South Church of Scotland, Aberdeen and beyond, mention has been made, particularly among my friends of the Crieff Brotherhood, of the struggles and afflictions of earlier years which doubtless were a preparation for one's vocation. In addition, interest has been expressed in how this preparation has been used in my life's work. Some have felt that much of this should be shared, both as an insight into God's dealing with a soul, bringing peace, fulfilment and a measure of fruitfulness, and also as an encouragement to others who may not yet see the Lord's purposes in their various doubts, defeats and periods of darkness. The volumes of The Gilcomston Story already published recount the greater part of my life which since 1945 has been closely bound to my calling as minister of Gilcomston. Yet it was felt that my own recollections on a broader level may be of usefulness to some. I pray that this is so. It was Martin Luther who once said that there are three things which make a minister: study, prayer and afflictions.

William Still
1991

Part
1

Unlikely
Lad

CHAPTER 1

ROOTS

The surname 'Still' is thought to be Anglo-Saxon in origin and rates mention in the Domesday Book. There is also record of a Henry Stylle de Saulton who made a donation in 1300 A.D. to Dryburgh Abbey in the Borders, and the first Still in Aberdeen was an Alexander Still who was a burgess of the city in 1451. So we go back a long way! By the beginning of the 17th Century there was quite a grouping of families of that name around the Oldtown of Aberdeen and in the Murcar, Belhelvie area. It was presumably from these that my family is descended. Certainly my great-great grandfather William Still married an Elspet Watson in 1793 from Belhelvie. They set up home in Newbridge in the Holburn area of Aberdeen where William was a surgeon/barber. Their elder children were all baptised in church by the successive ministers of Gilcomston Chapel of Ease, Rev. James Gregory and Professor James Kidd. Church baptisms were not very common in those days but this early connection with Gilcomston is naturally fascinating for me and interesting in the light of all we say about covenant baptism.

The family connections with the North East, and latterly with Aberdeen itself, continued. Firstly, my great-grandfather, Alexander, having been born in Aberdeen, lived in the Grampian village of Tarves where he began his apprenticeship as a shoemaker in the small community. At some point he moved to the coastal village of Gardenstown where he married Mary Jamieson in 1832. Of their nine children William, my grandfather, was born in 1841. By the time of the 1851 census Alexander was a master shoemaker. Yet the community was dominated by the fishing and his son, William became the local fish merchant. William, however, was a man of many skills and at one point built a house for his family, largely, I understand, with his own hands. It is a considerable three-storey erection made of solid granite, and for long was called the 'hoose at the hairbour'. It later became the property of my maternal grandfather's youngest brother, George West, and I have visited it and in my youth met its occupants, who were of Brethren persuasion, as many were in Gardenstown.

My memories of my paternal grandfather, William Still are, as I say, of a man of many gifts and of considerable stature both physically and personality-wise. He was a perfectionist, and was deeply irritated by shoddy work of any kind. It was said that in his old age when the family had already moved to Aberdeen to pursue the fish merchant's trade, there wasn't an employee who could put a nail in a box to please him (these were mostly one or two stone boxes for cured fish). I know that this is true, for on Saturday mornings as a little boy I used to repair to the fish-house on North Esplanade West by the river Dee and help put double lids on these boxes of fish, and woe betide me if the nail went through the side of the box and my grandfather came on the scene. Another great irritation of his was if any of us children put a foot on his prized flower beds.

The house I always associated with my grandparents was Beulah Villa. It stood on Albury Road in the Fonthill area of town and those precious flower beds of annuals ran on either side of the foot-walk to the front door. Wallflowers in the spring, and stocks, asters and calceolarias in the high summer were the invariable choice, which grandfather reared in seed boxes, and a brave show they made. The back garden was given over to vegetables, potatoes, etc., with a large patch of rhubarb and an ancient apple tree which produced the greenest, sourest apples you ever tasted - for apple jelly!

But before I arrive at my own youthful memories I must first tell of the family of my mother, Helen West. The Wests seem to have resided in Gardenstown for several generations, for with the name Watt, the Wests seem to have been the basis of the village stock. Gardenstown nestles practically under the twin cliffs of Mohr Head whose black rock face runs to several hundred feet of sheer drop, and Troup Head to the east, not so high, but jutting out much farther into the Moray Firth. Gardenstown's twin village was Crovie, which was simply one row of fisher cottages clinging to the shore under the shelter of Troup Head. Gardenstown was much the larger village, with its two churches, Parish and United Presbyterian, and another, the Parish Kirk of Gamrie, about a mile and a half inland.

It is said that before the Fifty-nine Revival, which John West, my grandfather, used to call the 'dancing revival' because of the excitement of the converts, Gardenstown was so lawless, fiercely independent and wild that the police from Macduff in the west or Fraserburgh in the east feared to enter the village. The revival changed all that, when whole families were converted, and Bible study, prayer, and the singing of Gospel hymns became the order of the day and night. Even outhouses used for stores of fishing gear were adapted as informal meeting-places. Many stories I recall from my mother and father of the revival meetings held in Castle Grant, a building apparently prodigiously old.

My grandfather, John West, was of course a fisherman as

were his two brothers, James and George. One of his first boats was called the *Jasper*, and doubtless that name came from the list of the jewels in the book of Revelation, and it indicates along with the names of many fishing vessels on that coast the supreme interest of the people in the Scriptures and the things of God. Later, when John's sons grew up, my uncles George, James, Frank and John, they called their vessels the *Golden West*, and there was, if I remember rightly, a second boat with the same name.

My maternal grandmother, Isabella Watt - called Donalie - McDonald being her maiden name, came from Crovie. She had a beloved sister, Jean, who was a great favourite of my mother's. She was a beautiful woman with an exceedingly chaste character, who died of cancer, and who on hearing what her mortal trouble was, declared that she did not know how she had contracted an 'unclean' trouble, she had always been so spotlessly clean - as fisher folk in the east of Scotland traditionally were. They kept their houses so clean and brightly painted that they often lived in sheds or outhouses during the summer months, not to 'blad' (spoil) their scrupulously kept and beautifully polished homes. My mother's mother was a highly intelligent woman, of great rectitude and discipline, perhaps stricter than she was loving. She trained her four sons and four daughters in every good habit. She was a remarkable provider, and during the summer months laid in stores of all kinds of nourishing foods for the winter. There was obviously a creative element in her nature which had, of course, little scope for outlet in that primitive environment, but which she made the best use of within her means and knowledge.

My mother, Helen, was the eldest of the four daughters, and was third in the family, George and James being her seniors. She had a particular love for her brother James, who seems to have had something of the same shy nature as my mother, but of course, marriage and families of their own naturally separated brothers and sisters somewhat. Yet until almost her dying day mother used to look back wistfully to the days when she and her brother James seemed to be particular chums. Whether he felt that in later life or not, is not known since he was a man of few words.

My mother being the eldest daughter was a great help to her mother and worked very hard to maintain the standards of the household, caring and catering for ten souls. In the early days of the family there seemed to be good relations between the sons and daughters. The four sons, George, James, Frank and John, remained in Gardenstown and the eldest three were intent, like practically all the rest of Gardenstown youth then on the fishing. But things changed and when my Uncle Frank had a nasty accident at sea and lost all the fingers of one hand, and I think, one of the other, he had to give up the sea, and bought a general merchant's store in the village. Soon the youngest son, John, with the youngest daughter, Bella, began to take an interest in the wider world, especially in art and music. John, however, was called up and killed in the First World War, within a month or two of its ending, in 1918. My mother's father never got over the loss of his youngest son and grieved, it is said, to the day of his death because he did not know if John, who had undoubtedly worldly interests, was saved.

The same artistic bent was present in all the four sisters. My Aunt Jeannie married a George Anderson from Macduff, 'one of nature's gentleman'. (He made friends with an Admiral during the First World War, who later gave him his yacht which became a fishing boat at Macduff for many years, with some of the fine appointments of such a beautiful craft in my Aunt's home - I have a table knife from it yet.) Aunt

Jeannie was a person with a great love of beauty of every kind
and devoted much time to the care and decoration of her
beautiful home at Garden Street, Macduff. My next aunt,
Elizabeth (Lizzie), who became a school teacher at Udny, and
subsequently married the local Joiner, David Wilkie, was the
'comedian' in the family, and in my childhood we used to look
forward to her week-end visits to our home in Aberdeen
where I was born.

My youngest aunt, Bella, had an even greater opportunity
for cultural education and training than Aunt Lizzie, and came
to Aberdeen to live with our family (as her favourite brother,
John, did) while she studied at Art School. She did carving,
pen painting, charcoal drawing and wonderful embroidery,
some of which I still have. Quite late in life Aunt Bella
married John Alexander, a local fisherman, a simple soul, but
a most likeable fellow who was a favourite with us all. It was
after he died that Aunt Bella came to live with our family in
Aberdeen at 31, Woodstock Road. Later, in 1945 when I
returned to Aberdeen from Glasgow to be minister of Gilcomston and needed a housekeeper for the manse at 18 Beaconsfield
Place, what should Aunt Bella do but sell up a small business
she owned and the cottage in Gardenstown which she had
retained and come to live with me. Thus the manse was first
furnished with her furniture, including many beautiful things.
It was a wonderful provision for me, since it was destined that
I remained unmarried. More of 'Auntie' later, but she looked
after me well for nearly five years, during which time she not
only bore the brunt of the new regime in Gilcomston, but
endeared herself to so many of the young converts of these
days that there used to be a stream of them, and older folk too,
calling at the manse - not to see the minister, but to sit at the
fireside in the back kitchen with Auntie and confide in her.

My father's family consisted of three sisters and himself,

an only son. All the sisters remained in the Grampian area as did their families. It has always been a great source of joy to me that at least one of my relations from this connection, young Moira, one of my cousins' daughters was brought up in Gilcomston. She later married Dr. Douglas MacDougall and her Christian profession and the godly way in which she and Douglas are bringing up their two adopted children, Martin and Alison, is a delight.

I am one of six surviving children. The oldest child, William whose name I was given, died at the age of nine months, from measles in 1904. His death was a cruel blow to my parents, and my mother often used to tell of the Sunday morning following the funeral how she went to Torry Church where they worshipped, to find the service already begun and the congregation singing, *Around the throne of God in heaven, thousands of children stand!* She said it nearly broke her heart. Until her death she kept a lock of her little child's hair: it was fair, and we often used to take it out and look at it. She kept it in what was really a hanging pocket of a soft grey colour which adorned her wedding dress. Our family thereafter consisted of my eldest sister Barbara, John my elder brother, myself, Helen (Ellie), David and Irene (Rene).

My father was a cooper to trade, as was his father before him, but both of them eventually left that trade for the herring industry itself, which had called for cooperage, and they became pioneers in it. In those days, fish merchants followed the herring fishing boats as they followed the shoals of herring during the summer, from Lerwick to Fraserburgh, and thence in the late Autumn to Lowestoft and Yarmouth. My mother as a young girl of fifteen or sixteen, said to be declining with what was then called 'consumption' (tuberculosis), was sent to Baltasound and Uyeasound on the island of Unst in Shetland to live in a hut during the summer and cook for the fishermen, her father and her brothers; the family made up the boat's crew themselves. The herring shoals moved south during the course of the year.

Fraserburgh was the main midsummer port for the herring fishing, while into the Autumn the herring shoals moved further south towards Yarmouth and Lowestoft. The exodus of the fishing boats during the months of September to November and even December was an invariable part of life in these days. It is strange how such patterns change, and none like them survive. Whether the herring still move in that direction, I cannot say, but an embargo having being placed on catching them lest the species die out, herrings and kippers have become almost unknown.

My father then followed in his father's footsteps and became a fish merchant, and with other support began a business in Shetland which did not prosper. There was some trouble about winding it up, the details of which, fortunately, I do not remember, but he then started in business with his brother-in-law, Charles Goodall, and that business was more successful. Eventually the partners separated, cordially as it happened, both being men of peace, and my father took the extensive premises at North Esplanade West which remained in the family business into the late 1970's, when my younger brother David sold them and, as the remaining member of the family still active in business, rented a smaller place.

CHAPTER 2

EARLY TROUBLES

During the family's sojourn in Aberdeen, my parents lived in many places, seven to be precise including a spell back in Gardenstown, and the various shifts mirror the fortunes and misfortunes with which my youth was punctuated. Their move to a home in Cults, however, coincided with the prospering of my father's fish merchant's business which allowed him the luxury of indulging his increasing interest in the new sport of motor-cycling, and then motoring. He is said to have possessed the first Sunbeam car in the district, a photograph of which taken at the Clatterin' Brig, Cairn-a-Mount, used to hang in our home. We have prints of it now.

But our life of considerable affluence was interrupted by the virtual collapse of the business, and it seemed, of my parent's marriage. It was all linked to my father's growing drink problem which was placing unbearable pressures upon both business and family life. As a child of five I was unaware of many of the details of this time but the point was reached when my mother was obliged to leave with her four children with Helen barely a toddler. Yet young as I was I well remember our departure from our lovely home. We went by train from Cults to Aberdeen, and thence to Macduff en route by bus to Gardenstown to our grandparents, West. I will never forget the journey. My brother John caught his finger in the train door at Cults, and so an injured boy simply added to the awful pathos in which we set out on a journey which was to lead practically to homelessness and poverty, and which tested to the full the resoluteness of my mother's character.

By then, the First World War was upon us of which my earliest awareness was a visit of my youngest uncle, John from the front line in 1915. It was my fourth birthday party but I remember the atmosphere changing as he brought the news that the *Lusitania* had been sunk on May 7th with all hands.

After the affluence of our various houses in Aberdeen and then in Cults came the poverty and separation of living with our grandparents in Gardenstown, our father having enlisted for military service. He joined the Motor Transport Corps on the advice of his friend William Meff, who later became Lord Provost of Aberdeen and was knighted. He remained a true friend to us. Father saw service in France and in Germany not being demobilised until 1919.

Our life in one room in High Street, Gardenstown, was rather miserable, and we five, two brothers, two sisters and mother, were practically on the poverty line. My father when on leave came to live with his sister, Elsie, and their garden overlooked the back entrance to our own room, and I have seen him standing there in his khaki uniform looking down to watch us. Eventually, although I began to go to school there, it was decided to return and find accommodation in Aberdeen. Finally at some time when my father was home on leave the family re-united, upon solemn promises of amended ways after demobilisation.

During our earlier years in the Ferryhill district of Aberdeen, and Cults, our parents had transferred their church membership from Torry Church to Ferryhill South, and then under the influence of William Meff to Trinity Church, Crown Street. I distinctly recall being taken to my first church service at Trinity - I must have been about three years of age.

Strangely enough it was the overwhelming sound of the organ and people singing lustily which frightened me, and I remember my mother dragging me out of church howling, to her great embarrassment. Later, I was baptised, not at church (it was not the practice then) but at Cults by the Rev. Thomas Angus Fraser, a well-known preacher at Trinity, to whose preaching and lectures students of these days flocked. However, when our home broke up, despite appeals by my Aunt Mary and my mother, Thomas Angus Fraser did nothing to help the situation, and my father was removed from the Church Roll.

Our first single room in Aberdeen on our return to the city was in Dee Street, and on returning we linked up with our former friends, the Lees whose father was also a fish merchant. Their children took us to the Salvation Army Citadel at Castle Street to which they belonged. They wore the uniform and the father and sons played in the band. Peter Lees was also Treasurer. This was our first contact with the Salvation Army which was to play such an important part in our youth.

We then moved to another single room in Chattan Place, which proved to be over-run with mice. I remember one awful night when our back kitchen seemed to be taken over by these horrid creatures, until we all took shelter in one bed including baby Helen, and my brother John kept the creatures away from the bed with a sweeping brush. Next morning my mother went to see the local Army Colonel who in the end gave her living quarters in the barracks, where we lived until my father was demobbed. These premises were just round the corner from my grandparents' home at Beulah Villa. My father, whose creative talents showed themselves in many practical ways, drew out plans to add another living room and scullery in the villa's extensive back garden, so that eventually we moved to that address and shared the now extended house with our grandparents and Aunt Mary. From there I attended school at Ferryhill. Then when the rule of zoning was introduced and children were obliged to attend their district school, we were sent to Holburn Street School, which we did not like, since the rather wild kids from the Hardgate went there. I soon graduated to the Secondary School at Ruthrieston, but from there went to Gordon's College, a fee-paying school which my brother John had attended.

The family fortunes improved upon my father's return to business. He was a clever man, and with his agile mind, could assess prices of fish in the market and work out his possible margin of profit before he bid for them. He was highly respected among the fish merchants' fraternity, and Peter Lees, John R. Stephen (whose daughter later became our family doctor) and William Meff were his good friends. I went to Gordon's College after my 13th birthday on the 3rd of September, 1924, but following a trip to Grantown-on-Spey with my sister Barbara on the September holiday late in the month a nervous trouble which had begun around the age of seven with its fierce itch, festerings and scabs resurged and I was not able to go to school on the Tuesday morning.

I never went back to school after that. Sent away to a farm in Tarland in the country, I remained there during the months of October, November and into December, my health improving somewhat, although the Spartan life of an Aberdeenshire farmhouse I found ungraceful and desolating. From the beginning of that year, 1925, I was simply at home, unable to go to school, and on my fourteenth birthday on the 8th of May it was agreed that I should follow my grandfather's, father's, and older brother John's footsteps into the fish trade, with, of course, very little education.

My nervous trouble, which mother always thought sprang

from strains at home - the problems with my father and the many moves which the family underwent - had begun with an extreme skin irritation. I had sulphur baths every day, and often was so covered with sores and festerings on the exposed parts of my body that it was not possible for me to go to school. I have gone to bed at night with my lips, hands, and knees all poulticed. The trouble seemed to clear by my mid-teens, but then developed into neuritis, which crippled my attempts to become a pianist, and then seemed to affect my equilibrium until it disrupted my life entirely for a number of years in my twenties.

CHAPTER 3

MORE TROUBLES

I was therefore a fish worker in my father's business for three years. At least, that was what I was supposed to be, but I hated the fish with its smells and the rigours of cold winter days heading cod and coming home with the smell of fish oozing from my pores. I soon ingratiated myself into the office, where John Carson, who had tried to maintain the business from the shelter of that cosy place during my father's absence at the war was in charge. How the business survived my father's absence, having been formerly almost on the rocks, I do not know, but against my father's will, who loved the cut and thrust of the fish market and whose elder son, John was training in that same school, I insisted myself into the office staff, and there I remained until another possibility opened up to me.

The only thing I seemed to be good at, and enjoyed, was piano playing. We all learned to play the piano, except brother John, who took to the violin. Our musical interests were fuelled by our continued involvement in the Salvation Army but I always preferred the piano and singing to the brass instruments which were the normal mode of music-making in the Army. Nonetheless, I learned to play the tenor horn in the Junior Band, then the baritone, and in the Senior Band, the trombone. It was even occasionally remarked that I produced a good tone on the tenor horn. Yet I advanced particularly in playing the piano and began to play in public. My old friend, Charles Dent, who was my Junior Band Leader at the Salvation Army, encouraged me by taking me out to meetings and concerts to accompany his fine singing voice. I accompanied him at the prison of Craiginches as soon as I was fourteen, and I remember playing my first piano solo in Cullen Town Hall when our Boy's Band spent a week-end on the Moray Firth, mostly at Buckie, Portessie and Findochty. On Monday evening we gave a performance in Cullen, and the local Provost, chairing it, on hearing me thump out Rachmaninoff's Prelude in C sharp Minor on a deplorable piano, said I would go far!

By seventeen I was thinking of piano teaching. I left The Salvation Army then and immediately became organist of the Methodist Church. My music teacher, Irvine Cooper, unknown to me up-dated my age, and I became a professional accompanist. At the same time, the family fortunes improved again and we moved to our own terraced house in the salubrious Queen's Cross district, and my father bought a Chapell Baby Grand piano for me. So I was a music teacher from 1928 until I left Aberdeen in 1934 for London. I had remained organist of the Methodist Church for over two years until I was nineteen, and devoted myself to music and the study of Handel, Bach, Beethoven, as my very life.

It was my dissatisfaction with Army music which really fuelled my departure from it at the age of seventeen but I was undoubtedly slipping away at this time from the commitment I had made to Christ when only thirteen. One instance actually sparked off my move and happened one Sunday at an Army open air meeting. We were holding the meeting in Albion Street behind the Citadel. It was nearing the close of the meeting and to my intense embarrassment the leader said, 'Brother Still will close in prayer.' I was transfixed with fear and couldn't open my mouth. When no words came the leader closed the meeting himself and I was left to put all my anger into my trombone as we marched to the hall for the afternoon meeting. So angry was I that I stubbed my foot on a granite set on the street and hurt my lip on the mouthpiece: that increased my fury at being so humiliated before all my cronies in the band.

When we got to the band room I said to the Band-leader, 'That's me finished!' (I can't remember if I played for the rest of that day but it was my last Sunday with the Salvation Army until, a rather different character, I returned at the age of nineteen.)

Having obtained the position of organist at the Methodist Church my rebellion showed itself in that although I played in the church I reacted against all things spiritual. I even resolved not to listen to a word the minister said! Judge how foolish this was since my first minister there was Vincent Taylor, who later became Principal of Headingly College, Leeds, and one of the most respected New Testament scholars of his day. His successor was Herbert Benson, a very gracious man, whose elder brother became President of the Methodist Conference.

However, I became increasingly lonely during my years as a private Music Teacher and organist of a church where there was little youth fellowship. Having come from the Salvation Army which was always milling with young people, I missed their company. I also began to realise that I was running away from God. Yet, like the Hound of Heaven he is, he was pursuing me relentlessly. Finally, sitting at the organ one winter's night very late, in a cold church, the Lord spoke to me as plainly as ever I heard, and said, 'Go and resign from this post and go back to The Salvation Army where you belong.' I did just that: the resignation was duly posted, and

Herbert Benson called to confirm that I meant it, and back to
The Salvation Army, its uniform, bands, music, I went. More
importantly, I had listened to the voice of God and was going
back to him.

Almost at once I was appointed Songster Leader, and
embarked on a career of choir training in earnest. Music still
tended to predominate, I fear, but under the influence of two
godly Salvation Army Officers, Percy Collins and Thomas
Heath, the latter becoming my youngest sister Rene's father-
in-law, I grew more and more devoted to the Lord and his
service. I started to go to Public Houses on Saturday nights
with the *War Cry*, and finally offered myself for training for
officership. I knew the Lord was calling me to his service, and
where else would I serve than in the Army, where I was so
happy?

The family moved house yet again to a newly-built bunga-
low in town in July and I entered the William Booth Memorial
Training College at Denmark Hill near Camberwell in London in August 1934. I gave myself to the Lord in that holy
place and felt that this would be my life. I was determined to
fulfil my calling. However, all did not go as planned. A certain
nervousness and shyness and an intense introspection seemed
to dog me. There was something wrong that I could not
fathom and could not shake off. Studying became a strain
although *I* felt that I was becoming daily more holy and
committed. I really thought I was well on the way to becoming
a 'saint'. I became exceedingly ascetic, and wrote home to
advise my family not to send the goodies they lavished on me
although the fare at the College was very plain. By the
Christmas vacation I was growing more and more strained
and nervous, and less inclined to take my due, voluntary part
in open-air activity etc. Yet still I believed that I was becoming
a purified and more holy person. That belief was very sincere,

but I recall my first day home in Aberdeen, taking a walk out King's Gate towards Hazlehead, I saw something which stirred such a fierce bout of temptation within me that I received a very great shock, and realised that, out of my hot-house I was as vulnerable as ever to carnal temptation, and that holiness was not a safe and sure plane that one could attain and remain on permanently without effort. How inadequate for life was the teaching on holiness I had imbibed!

My week's Christmas vacation was far too short. Under the influence of home and its relaxations I had almost collapsed, and was granted a further week's sick leave. Even so, I returned reluctantly, feeling in every sense weak.

Yet the return to college was marked by two remarkable circumstances which often puzzled me. Arriving at King's Cross early one morning I made my way to College and found that, being expected, every cadet in my house had taken their mats from their rooms and laid them in the corridor to form a carpet for me to walk on, and each man stood to attention to provide a guard of honour for my entrance. I couldn't believe it. On asking why, I was told that the cadets on returning had been asked to nominate the cadet who had most influenced them in their first term, and the overwhelming vote had gone to me. It seemed the most extraordinary thing when during the latter part of that term I was agonising all the time that I might have strength and courage just to carry on until the Christmas vacation. Of course I made friends, but I was not aware of being any particular influence for good. I can only conclude that my sincere desire to follow the Lord and give up all for him, along with my appalling sense of weakness, had allowed something to come forth that meant more to my fellow-cadets than I was aware of. However, it took less than a fortnight for me to see that I was simply not capable of going on. There was every kind of weakness, except that the Lord was even closer to me than ever, and it was he one day who plainly said, 'Yes, William, you can go home, you're not well.' It was a shock to staff and cadets alike, and I had an interview with the Principal, Samuel Hurren who was kind, and who agreed that I should return home. It was not easy to do so. My elder sister, Barbara, who loved the Army, and had been grieved when I left it at the age of seventeen had paid for my complete rig-out of uniform when I returned two and a half years later. She was so proud that I was to be a Salvation Army Officer, and that hope being dashed affected her deeply. Both she and the rest of the family were determined to do all they could to help me back to health and strength.

But what was wrong? No medical examinations could find anything organically wrong and psychiatrists in those days were only for insane people. Although I was admittedly inturned and moody and withdrawn, I was not insane - except that nerves overtook me until I could not sleep, and in fact did not really sleep for months on end. I even used to stand at my bedroom window overlooking the city and the bay, and wonder if I should jump through the window and end it all. I wanted to die, and thought many times in my misery of how I might take my miserable life. But I could not jump through that window because of the words of Scripture, particularly the words of an anthem we used to sing in the Army long ago, 'Thou wilt keep him in perfect peace whose mind is stayed on thee, because he trusteth in thee.' There wasn't any peace, of course, let alone perfect peace then but these words kept me holding on to life, without any sense of purpose, just holding on, nakedly and barely, purposelessly in a sense, as it seemed then. I found no joy in anything or anyone, could not concentrate, could not bear to meet people outside the family circle, and became a recluse, trying to do some hand work in the winter and weeding the garden in the summer, almost

endlessly. What was wrong with me? I recall hearing my
mother say when I left school for good at the age of thirteen
that I might never be of much use, but the family would have
to be good to me! It seemed as true of me in my mid-twenties!

By November 1935 my mother, completely distracted by
my continuing weakness and inability to concentrate, confided in her neighbour, Mrs. Douglas, a Brethren woman from
Gourdon, who lived across the street. She said her daughter
had tried many doctors with some complaint which I do not
remember, but none could help her, and she had been advised
to go to Glasgow to a Dr. Brown Hendry, a godly homeopathic
physician. My mother said she would take me anywhere in the
world if only I could be cured. So one dark November
morning I was almost carried into our V.8 Ford car and taken
to Glasgow to see this man. I can never forget it. He asked me
questions which seemed of a psychological nature, but also
about my likes in food, etc. After writing down a good deal
he looked up at me with his kindly professional air and said
firmly, 'If you take my medicine I will make a new man of
you.' It was all so simple and matter-of-fact, but I believed
that man implicitly, and left his consulting room with some
words of spiritual counsel, and went home to begin to return
to health.

CHAPTER 4

REFLECTIONS

I must pause here and recall some of the experiences of the first twenty-four years of my life and consider what factors in heredity and environment contributed to them. I think my parents and their stock were markedly stronger in the creative than in the rational elements of life, although my father had an excellent mind for figures and mathematics. Mother was always inclined to believe that the throes of our family life with its disruptions and upsets had left a deeper imprint on me than on the other children, thus causing my physical troubles. Certainly I had more trouble with my health in my childhood and youth than the others. This was pronounced to the extent that I suppose I was always regarded as the sickly one and a bit of an odd-bod among the others, and most often on my own.

I certainly grew up with both a great sense of inadequacy: a fear of life and of growing up and becoming a responsible adult. But as was perhaps not unnatural in the circumstances, I was a bit of a dreamer with a vaulting ambition, and often painted to myself glowing pictures of what I wanted to become. I recall that during my College days in The Salvation Army we cadets were discussing our ambitions, and one fellow said that he did not want to be anything more than a humble Captain of a local Corps, when I piped up and said, 'Nothing less than the General for me!' It was said light-heartedly but there was truth in it, too. I did want to be somebody, for I felt certain powers within me, especially of thought, and yet it was not so much what I would call rational thought. I do not think that I was more than average at school when I was well enough to attend, but occasionally hit the high spots if the subject appealed to me. Indeed an old teacher of mine still alive in her nineties protests that I was above average. However, I still think that I was defective in the kind of clear thought which made for efficiency in so many areas of thought and life.

Much later on, Ian Lawson one of the ablest young men who has passed through Gilcomston, once said to me that I often jumped to the right conclusion which took him a whole process of rational thought to reach. He meant that as a compliment, but I knew that I had often 'jumped' to the wrong conclusion, in which case a process of rational thought which was not so much in my line, would have reached the right conclusion.

Be that as it may, being an intuitive and an emotional creature, rather than a rational one, what could I do but make the best of what I was and am. Roy Campbell, presently of Stirling University, once said I could never be an academic and I knew he was right. That is not to say that I have not done a great deal of rational thinking, but it has often been arduous and even irksome, and I have often used my wits rather than my brains to protect myself, and to afford me an air of being more intelligent, or, at least, intellectual than I am.

I suppose it is true to say that I largely dreamed away my childhood and early youth, and it was only in later years when I had to come to terms with manhood that I sought to bring my dreams down to the realms of reality.

It was undoubtedly the interest in music and some gift in it that began to give me confidence that there was something

I could do. My mother's family was far more musical than my father's. My paternal grandmother, Mary Lawrence, used to say that the worst about going to church was the awful noise of the organ! The fright I mentioned earlier on hearing the organ at Trinity was probably prior to the occasion when we lived at Cults when I grabbed a hymn book and went out to the garden and, standing by a clothes-rope standard, imagined I was at church and sang away to myself possibly with the book upside-down, until I became aware that the family were at the window killing themselves with laughter. I was certainly intrigued from then onwards with the thought of going to 'turch'. Landing in The Salvation Army at the age of five of course also gave encouragement to musical activity of various kinds.

At the age of sixteen I was taking organ lessons as I have mentioned from Irvine Cooper, the gifted organist of Ferryhill South Church, who was also known for his masterly handling of the massive Music Hall organ, and at seventeen I was made organist of the local Methodist Church. It was my responsibility to be Choir Master as well as Organist, and I had some experienced choristers who had sung for years with Arthur Collingwood in the Aberdeen Choral Union and were experts in the sol-fa notation. Collingwood, incidentally, was later my organ teacher when I practised on the Langstane organ across the road from Gilcomston, and later still when Collingwood became Professor of Music at Saskatoon University, Canada, Marshall Gilchrist of St. Machar's Cathedral became my piano and organ teacher.

As a Choir Master at the helpless age of seventeen I had to learn something about singing and so I set to study it with a will. I knew I hadn't a solo voice, so instead of going to a singing teacher I grabbed all the books on singing I could find in the Public Library and devoured them. One of the best was

the book on choral singing by Sir Henry Coward, conductor
of the famous Huddersfield Choral Society, and then a book
on singing technique by an Italian with a name like 'Marchetti'.
I studied the technique and used to go out to the country and
walk the roads and lanes away from everybody practising my
singing, including breathing, preserving an open throat, with
that 'yawning feeling' which is the essence of relaxation, and
taking a line of a hymn and practising diction with emphasis
upon the consonants, d's, t's, n's, m's, p's, s's and diphthongs.

At the same time I was becoming a professional accompanist and played at concerts and dinners as well as beginning
to teach the piano and to immerse myself in the life of a young
musician. Yet although I had reacted against following Christ
at seventeen in favour of this life, a large part of the reason for
my return to my earlier commitment was due to the fact that
I became disillusioned with a life which seemed to contain
only music. Even as I concentrated on my music and practising the organ until the latest hours of the coldest nights, I was
aware that all was not well. I should also say that during my
sojourn at the Methodist Church my choir had given a
programme of music at the Army's Sunday afternoon Family
Gathering. When I finally returned to the Army my friends
there remembered this and so I became Songster Leader.
Thus, having equipped myself for the task through the
enforced self-teaching and the experience at the Methodist
Church, I proceeded to raise the Army Songsters' Brigade to
a new level of choral singing, especially unaccompanied. I
continued in this work while also music teaching for four
years from the age of nineteen, the Lord progressively taking
a grip on me until the clear call to full-time work as an Officer
in The Salvation Army had to be answered.

It intrigues me now to think that early in 1934 when the
Candidates' Secretary, Col. Handel Boot, came to Aberdeen

to interview me, an evening meeting was held in Gilcomston South Church, when I conducted our Songsters. However, we were not allowed to touch the organ since the organist at that time was Mr. Wood, a rather forbidding character who for obvious reasons was known as 'Tarzan'. (Years later in 1945 when as minister of Gilcomston South I first had opportunity to sit at its organ and produce its glorious strains, I recall saying to myself, 'See me now, Monkey Wood!') By the month of August 1934 I was off to London to the International College of The Salvation Army at Denmark Hill.

But to return to my teens, I recall that other interests which bolstered my increasing obsession with music began to show themselves. Indeed, it was impossible to read and study so widely in music and singing without partly educating myself in other subjects. Perhaps the earliest stimulation to anything of a literary nature was the challenge of my music master Irvine Cooper to study musical history. He gave me a book on George Frederick Handel - a wise choice - and asked me to write an essay on it. I had also heard Irvine Cooper give a lecture in his church hall on Grieg, the Norwegian composer which fascinated me and so I began to read under his direction and then very tentatively put pen to paper. I filled a good sized exercise book after chiselling my sentences over and over again, and handed it to him. He professed astonishment - I did not know what he expected, or I expected, but I thought he rather flattered me about what he called 'my literary gift'. But that did something to me, along with my developing musical education, to help me believe that odd-bod and rather sickly soul though I was, I might be of some use yet.

I recall that five years later in 1934 when at the Army College I presented essays on books of my choice which we were required to read and write upon (one was John Bunyan's *Grace Abounding*) I was given the highest mark, and a rather

superior fellow came to ask why I should gain such high
marks. He asked to read my essays. He had a little more
respect for me after that! You see, he mixed with the
intellectuals whereas my friends were mostly rather ordinary
chaps. Indeed, one of our sergeants took me to task for not
making the right friends in the College. What he thought
when many had publicly acknowledged me as a particular
influence on their lives (on my return from extended Christmas leave owing to ill-health) I don't know, but twenty-five
years later I met him at a Salvation Army Rally in the Royal
Albert Hall, London, where my brother-in-law Norman Heath
was singing a solo. Sadly, this chap tried to tell me, despite
what I said about the Lord blessing me in Gilcomston, that I
had got out of the Lord's will by leaving the Army. I recall
that two other officers when I finally came home sick in
January 1935, hinted at the same thing, one saying I had put
my hand to the plough and turned back. Later, one of these
men became a rank backslider, and I met him in Westburn
Road, Aberdeen, in khaki uniform and he looked through me.
I had earlier written to him at Peterhead reminding him of
what he had said, and how sorry I was that he had abandoned
the faith, and he wrote back a cryptic note telling me to mind
my own business.

In those days of course, it was ingrained in us that the
churches were practically all dead, and that is why God raised
up William Booth and The Salvation Army. Other break-
away groups from earlier days than the beginnings of The
Salvation Army were inclined to say the same, but they in their
turn have suffered a certain amount of deadening. Even so
they have refused to believe that any good thing could come
out of the auld, dead Kirk. What they did not realise was that
the same auld dead Kirk still held, at least formally, to her
Westminster Confession of Faith, and paid lip service to it at

ordinations and inductions. When another generation arose, which began to know the Lord, and turned to look at the Church's origins, she proved to have powers of recovery far beyond what break-away groups could believe. The fact that she has powers of recovery has subsequently been abundantly proved, as many ministers in the Church of Scotland, and many more conservative evangelical ministers coming up, have demonstrated.

A strong element in my personality and temperament as I say was emotional and aesthetic perhaps more than rational, and this was fed by life in The Salvation Army, whose life following the Booth family was of a demonstrative, dramatic and even theatrical nature. There is, of course, in religion that element too, as the fact that miracle plays, opera, and drama itself were largely born from the Scriptures, and it is no surprise to me that The Salvation Army have turned to these forms of expression and communication increasingly in latter years. The Army always loved dressing up, and now with make-up, stage scenery and a high standard of acting combining with their excellent brass bands and latterly guitar bands such as the former Joy Strings, they have made a name for themselves.

It is interesting to me to note that one of the Joy Strings was Bill Davidson, the son of one of the prominent Davidson family in The Salvation Army Citadel in Aberdeen in my youth. His father is Lieut. Col. William Davidson, the boyhood chum of my brother, John, and his mother Nan Walker, a dear friend of my youth.

It must be noted, however, that for all that I now know my place is to be in the national church, it was on my return to the Salvation Army from the Methodist Church that I began to grow spiritually. Under the influence of The Salvation Army Officers of that time, Herbert Betts, William Walsh, an

Ulsterman, and particularly Percival Collins, and having found an evangelical barrenness in the Methodist Church, I began to combine my music and choral work with a renewed interest in spiritual things. Prayer, including 7 a.m. knee drill on Sunday mornings before a full day's activities, Bible Reading and taking part in the more specifically spiritual aspect of Army Life became a major preoccupation of my years from the age of nineteen to twenty-three. Our Songster Brigade during that time became something of a spiritual as well as a musical influence both on our own Corps, and to others on occasional excursions beyond Aberdeen.

Then came my application to be accepted for training as a Salvation Army Officer convinced that the Lord was calling me to his service. As stated before, my Cadetship lasted from August 1934 to January 1935 when my nervous trouble, whatever the cause, got the better of me, and I came home to vegetate miserably until November of that year. It was then that under the influence of a godly neighbour my parents were prevailed upon to take me to Glasgow to the homeopathic doctor, James Brown Hendry, of Queen's Park, who gave me hope. I then began very painfully to work my way back to normality. These were tortured years from 1935 through 1936 to 1937, years which included the growing Hitler threat, the death of George V, the abdication of Edward VIII, and the coronation of George VI in 1937.

CHAPTER 5

NEW HOPE

It must have been towards the end of 1937 that I began to feel definitely the good effects of my homeopathic treatment, with periodic visits to my Glasgow doctor for check-ups and encouragement. I am sure that I owe my life, certainly my sanity, to this man, and I am undyingly grateful to him and to his son, Raymond, who succeeded him in the practice, and is still my homeopathic doctor.

One of my visits to Dr. Brown Hendry was combined with a trip for us children in our family caravan. (My father must have built at least seven or eight caravans with his own hands, and at one time practically every stick of furniture in our house was made and French-polished by him - I think he only stuck at upholstery!) On that family holiday we visited the great British Empire Exhibition at Bellahouston Park, Glasgow. That was an occasion! We caravanned at Thornliebank, and toured the exhibition which contained many wonders, and indeed reflected something of the twilight of the British Empire.

I recall that Charles Laughton, the famous character actor, with his wife Elsa Lanchester, were there that day, and we heard Laughton recite in the open air a speech from one of the Henry plays of Shakespeare which asserted national independence at a time in the Spring of 1938 when the threat from Hitler concerning the Sudetenland, Czechoslovakia, Austria and Poland was developing. Laughton was given a great ovation, for he stirred patriotic feelings which were very much needed during the subsequent years of the Second World War.

With regard to the years of my illness from 1935 to 1938 I have of course little documentation and have not been able to determine some of the significant dates within that period. I have already said that it was towards the end of 1937 that I really began to feel better, but the friend of my youth, James Goodrum, assures me that I resumed my post as Army Songster Leader early in 1936. If I undertook these duties as early as 1936 I can hardly think they were very well performed, because I was exceedingly withdrawn and feared to face people.

It must have been during 1936 that the Divisional Commander of The Salvation Army for North East Scotland, Brigadier Narraway, wanted to encourage me in Christian ministry beyond music and invited me to accompany him and Mrs. Narraway to the Fraserburgh Corps for a week-end of meetings. Mrs. Narraway promised that I would only be asked to play the piano, and not to speak. However, judge of my dismay and mental paralysis when at the beginning of the Saturday evening meeting she announced, 'Brother Still will pray.' It was a repeat of my humiliating experience at the age of seventeen. I immediately froze and could no more have opened my mouth than fly in the air. There was a long, embarrassed silence, and Mrs. Narraway meekly took the prayer herself, and was profuse with apologies afterwards. She had little idea, the dear woman, what that did to me.

There was another occasion, and I cannot find the date, when the Assurance Songsters came to Aberdeen from London - they were the crack Salvation Army Choir - and I was told that at the tea given to them on the Sunday afternoon I

would need to say a word of welcome. That worried me for
days. In the event I managed to get on my feet and as a
precaution said that I had been suffering from mental aberra-
tions and if my mind seized up I would have to sit down.
However, I must have been improving by then, for I was able
to say quite a bit which encouraged me no end. The particular
remark I made that remains with me was to the effect that in
choral work to preserve the balance of parts from chord to
chord one needed to indicate to the inner parts, alto, and tenor,
when they should be prominent and when not. I had been
training our Songsters this way, and so was able to commend
this fine choir from London for their consistent balance and
beautiful chording, not to say their crystal clear diction.

Whenever I resumed my leadership of the Songster Brigade, I was certainly active when my sister Rene's father-in-
law, Thomas Heath came to Aberdeen Citadel from Clapton
Congress Hall, London, in October, 1936. By then, I was
sufficiently recovered from my sickness and emerging from
under the cloud of sub-rational thought and the perpetual
mental 'toothache' which I had suffered these years, to take
a more active interest in the general work of the Army, and
consider the possibility of applying again to enter training for
Officer-ship.

The years from 1936 to 1938 were certainly intensely
spiritual for me in my leadership of the Songsters, yet my
earlier spell of leadership on returning to the Army from the
Methodist Church in the 1930's was probably more marked
for its spiritual content. Then I had naturally had a new surge
of interest in spiritual things, and under the inspiring ministry
of Percy Collins and his able devoted wife, the Songsters had
become a spiritual as well as a musical force. It was then that
I became almost fanatical for diction, keeping saying to them
that since they were singing the Gospel every word must be

clearly heard. I recall that years later when we had a Children's Choir in Gilcomston, I used to say to them that they were to imagine that there was a deaf old lady in the back gallery - deaf people always sit as far away as possible! - and their diction had to be clear enough for her to hear every word.

At that time the spiritual had often taken precedence over the musical. It was in those days after a fire occurred in Aberdeen Citadel which destroyed a good part of the roof of the hall that the Corps found shelter in the vacated Trinity Church at the foot of Marischal Street. Although accommodation there was cramped, these days contained some of the most spiritual experiences I recall in the Army. Nevertheless, I always consider the work in the later years from 1936 to 1939 under the ministry of Thomas Heath as a spiritual 'high', for me at least as I emerged from under a cloud of illness into greater stability and strength.

The emphasis in my work with the Songsters from 1936 to 1938 lay increasingly in the area of the demonstrative. In special musical meetings we began to include dramatic musical productions which were, I suppose, the precursors of the present Salvation Army series of biblical operas which are engaging the minds of their musical forces increasingly. What we did was to enact the stories which had inspired certain well known hymns. For instance, Jacob at Bethel, while the Songsters sang *Nearer my God to Thee* to the impressive tune, Horbury. Another piece of drama concerned the evangelical hymn *Behold Me standing at the door* when one of our songsters appeared in a thoroughly worldly setting while a hand appeared knocking outside her door. It was the Saviour's hand, and her reactions during the singing of the hymn conveyed their own challenging appeal. Yet another dramatic presentation which I fear went to extremes, took the evening hymn *At even when the sun was set* and enacted a

Middle Eastern scene in which we also used Albert Ketelbey's *In a Persian Market*. That piece describes a whole day in the life of a Persian market and so we 'went to town' in presenting this, using our wide platform to fine effect. It was after the hullaballoo had subsided in the evening hour that the sick were brought out and a figure representing the Saviour passed by and healed.

It was interesting that a year or two later when I had begun University studies and was appointed Organist of the Gallowgate Church, we planned to do the same Persian Market scene at a week-night concert with my Children's Choir. The children's homes were robbed of all sorts of materials including beads and bed-covers to dress the scene, but on the night of the dress rehearsal in the Gallowgate Church Hall, a German bomb was dropped on the Loch Street Bar. Although the Hall windows were blacked-out, the glass in the windows was sucked out and there was near panic, parents rushing in to retrieve their children. That was the end of the Persian Market, and dear Sibi Stephen, who was our pianist did not have the opportunity to show her flair for dramatic presentation.

* * * * * *

These dramatic presentations were admittedly spiritual in their appeal, and there was no doubt that as my health slowly improved I began to direct my thoughts more and more away from things merely musical to things spiritual. It must have been during the Spring of 1938 before we attended the Glasgow Exhibition that Commissioner Albert Osborne, the Army teacher and poet (he wrote the chorus, *Turn your eyes upon Jesus*) came to do a week-end at Aberdeen Citadel. The Songsters were in good fettle and their singing certainly added a spiritual dimension to the worship.

After one of the Sunday meetings I tackled the Commissioner about re-applying to the Army to enter training again, since I felt music was not really my calling, but some kind of spiritual ministry. He was kind about my work as a Songster Leader, but said the Army would not be prepared to risk accepting me to have another breakdown in health. I was doing good work where I was, he said, and should accept it as my service for the Lord. In saying this he ignored two factors: first, I had not worked for any remuneration since I gave up music teaching to enter the Army College in August 1934 and I could not live forever on my parents, generous though they had been to me; second, the Lord was definitely calling me to his service. So I said, 'Well, sir, if the Army won't have me, I'll have to seek his service elsewhere.' Whereupon rather peremptorily he said, 'Oh, Still, that kind of talk does not go down with me!' The Commissioner obviously regarded my words as a mere threat.

Next day, no less, a Monday, I went to see the Rev. MacKenzie Grieve of John Knox Gerrard Street Church of Scotland (I had heard him preach in the Army, and had met him elsewhere) about the possibility of entering the Church of Scotland ministry. The Church of Scotland was the obvious choice for me: outside of the Army I was blissfully ignorant of any theological debate and had no inkling of the degrees and shades of Christian opinion. The national Church seemed the only real alternative. In addition, I was aware that there was a college in Aberdeen and in my recuperative state I still required to live at home. Rev. MacKenzie Grieve received me kindly and sent me to Professor G. D. Henderson of the Chair of Church History, who advised me how to set about preparing. I said to him that I had left school for good at the age of thirteen, and had therefore had little formal schooling. He kindly said that I had doubtless learned much during these

years - I was 27 - but that for entrance examinations I needed
specific knowledge of particular things, including English
and languages. He sent me to a Tutor, Mr. Bremner, who
guided me in my study of the prescribed works for the English
Prelim in August: they were Shakespeare's *Macbeth*, Edmund
Burke, Scott's *Old Mortality*, and Milton's *Paradise Lost,
Book 1*.

Mr. Bremner said realistically that I hadn't a hope of
getting the English Prelim in August but I should try nonetheless. Meantime I had left the Army and begun the lonely task
of going round churches to hear what was being said. In
August of that year, 1938, I sat that Prelim, and to my great
astonishment and delight, passed it. Possibly it was the
required essay that helped me pass that exam, but during the
early summer months I certainly swotted hard these four
books and I think I knew them as I had never known books
before.

I could never say what that Preliminary success did to boost
my trembling ego. I felt inches taller and immediately embarked on study for my next qualification for entrance to the
modified course for the Church of Scotland ministry, the
subjects being Latin and Greek. I worked the rest of 1938 and
into 1939, the year of our country's fateful involvement in the
Second World War, and that summer I managed to pass them
both. That autumn there was also the requirement of an
examination on a number of books of the English Bible. It was
easier, and I studied hard and passed it also. Having passed
these exams I must have attended some selection interviews
but they cannot have been too exacting or stressful for I
remember nothing of them now. However, I was accepted
and it was as a candidate for the Church of Scotland ministry
that I was ready to enter the University of Aberdeen.

I should say that these studies, to a mind just emerging from the mental and emotional cloud I had been under for more than four years was a great trial. I am sure I would never have endured the strain of it had it not been for the sure conviction that the Lord was leading me into his service. Of course to begin with, my non-Salvation Army life was very lonely, for I missed the wonderful comradeship of the Army and the close fellowship of its musical sections. I did not find such fellowship anywhere in the churches as I had found in the Army, but coincident with my leaving the Army the organist of Gallowgate Church was advertised. It was only a glorified harmonium, but I got the post and during my student years had the joy of association with these dear people and making many Christian friends, some of whom I treasure to this day.

CHAPTER 6

UNIVERSITY

Now I want to recount my five years at Aberdeen University training for the ministry and my year as Assistant Minister in Glasgow. I have no intention of going beyond these years in this chronological account but will cover the subsequent years, of which Gilcomston is practically the whole of it, in the second part of this book which appears in a more topical form. The four volumes of *The Gilcomston Story* now extant already provide a more detailed, month-by-month record of these later years.

Yet to relate the happenings of even my student and assistantship years is a major task, and I address myself to it with some misgiving. I have gone through my lecture note-books and essays as well as scribblings on the former in an effort to determine chronology, but I think I have only achieved some semblance of order of the events.

Having passed all the preliminary examinations by the summer of 1939 I was ready to commence University studies in October, just after the War started. It was, then, under the shadow of that awful event that I entered a new world. One thing that greatly relieved me since my health was far from good, was that as a Divinity student I was exempt from military service, even if I had passed the medical test. Actually, I did not pass the medical test in respect of Cadetship in the University Officers' Training Corps. I hoped that if our nation survived at all (we exceedingly feared Hitler then) I would pursue my studies, and not have to wait for five to six years to the end of the war to undertake training for the ministry. In that case I would only have been starting to train at the time I was called to Gilcomston South Church, in the spring of 1945.

I will never forget my first lecture at University. In my first two years of Arts subjects before three full years of Divinity, I took First Year English, and with the smattering of Greek I had picked up the previous year, First Year Greek. That was more than enough for me, especially the Greek. I found myself plunged into a class which included five or six young men all of whom eventually graduated with First Class Honours. (One of them was Scott Couper, later Rector of Forres Academy and a good friend whose wedding service I conducted in Gilcomston in December 1946 when he married one of our young women, Jean Alison Reid.)

But, that first English lecture! As I sat in the large English lecture room in New King's with about a hundred other students practically all ten years younger than I (I was 28) and as I listened to Professor Bickersteth's first lecture of the session, I was aware that I had entered a new world, a world of wider knowledge. I almost scratched myself to make sure that it was real. I was actually a University student! But I was not without unmixed feelings, for I knew I had embarked on a career which would set me at least a little apart from ordinary folk with whom I had associated most of my life, for even as a Salvationist and young professional musician I had still felt myself to be one of the people.

Now, in a curious sort of way, I felt I had begun to climb into another category of human experience in which I would at last have an inbuilt advantage, separating myself from ordinary people. And although I was thrilled to be a University student, there was both a lingering regret that I had needed to climb on to such a bandwagon to attain my object of serving the Lord (did one need a University education to serve the Lord?). And so, not a little mild guilt welled up within me that I had betrayed my plebeian status.

I have these English notes now. The first lectures swept through practically the whole of human history, and I remember being thrilled at seeing history spread before me in a panorama, the difference between ancient and modern history being that in the old world, God was at the centre, whereas in the modern world, Man had taken the centre: this was set forth in a diagram on the board. So it went on until in literature we were into Chaucer (14th cent.), Shakespeare (16th), Milton (17th), Pope (18th), Wordsworth and Tennyson (19th).

Later, in my second year, doing History, I came across the following introductory paragraph to an essay on Erasmus which further brings out this point. It began:

Perhaps the unpardonable sin for one enjoying the privilege of University education would be to condone or excuse ignorance; and while those who are nurtured in learning and culture have the advantage of a broader and more liberal outlook, there is one blessing among the lamentable, and to some extent irreparable disadvantages of scholastic impoverishment in early years: it is the slow dawning of knowledge, and the realisation of the vastness of the world, of the kaleidoscopic past, the joy of studying incident, event, and trend, and of their appraisal in perspective and analysis, seeking for the underlying motives of those who make the events that make history - all in the light of maturer experience.

So I moved between the English classroom and that

dreaded smaller Greek classroom where I felt so much like a fish out of water; and although I made friends in the casual sort of way that young people do (one of them was John Gibb who later became minister of Olrig in Caithness) it was a lonely few months until I happened to meet Alex Crockett, first year Civil Engineering, and a keen member of Torry United Free Church.

Alex told me about the Christian Students' Fellowship (the C.S.F.) and that they met on Friday evenings and had a Prayer Meeting in the Students' Union on Saturday mornings. I decided to go, and from then on life assumed a more familiar colour, since I found myself among like minds. It was there that I met so many friends who for long thereafter were significant to me. There were Edward and Margaret Ingram, both in Medicine, whose biblical fundamentalism was an eye-opener to an ex-Salvationist. In those early days I learned very much from them, and from their Brethren background. There was Kenneth MacKenzie of the Free Church who eventually came over to the Church of Scotland and married Margaret Torrance. Kenneth went to Africa as a missionary and on returning to Parish work in Edinburgh died, greatly lamented, at a remarkable early age. There was Betty Patience, Maggie White (later Roy Miller's wife), and Donald McDonald, a medic who became Secretary of the C.S.F. and returned to his native Stornoway, where he remained as a doctor until his death some time ago. We had been good friends.

It was, as I remember, the next Easter, 1940, that I went with a large contingent of Aberdeen students to the Inter-Varsity Fellowship Conference at Bonskeid. There I met Tom Torrance, a speaker that year, Alexander Ross, the Free Church Minister who had been minister at Dee Street Free Church, Aberdeen, and Douglas Johnston, General Secretary of the I.V.F., who waged cordial but earnest warfare with

Tom Torrance on his Barthianism - 'the badness of goodness'.

I recall that as we walked to the country church for the evening service that Sunday, Tom had said to his companion that he had two sermons in his pocket and did not know which he would preach. In the event, what he did preach, was drier than his talk to the students, and that to me was very different from the spontaneity of an Army meeting to which I had been accustomed - not that a Salvation Army Officer would not prepare his message, but it would never be a matter of two manuscripts with almost a toss-up as to which it would be! That Easter was exceedingly cold and we men students were relegated to an auxiliary building at Bonskeid with absolutely no heating whatsoever. We were glad when it came to meal times to enter the big house. But it was a wonderful week-end, and photographs of it recall to me many who were around in the evangelical scene then, and some of them for long after that.

Despite the War situation worsening, the long summer vacation afforded me opportunities for Christian work in the Gallowgate Church with dear Archie Inglis, the Minister, who had been in the Royal Household Cavalry. He had since been a missionary with London City Mission, and subsequently a Church of Scotland Minister, doing the same Modified Course I was undertaking. Being still in a state of some mental aberration but improving, I welcomed the long summer break to ease and rest my mind. Yet I had the satisfaction of knowing that although all the Modified Course required was to fulfil the Class work with its examinations at Christmas and Easter, I had dared to sit the English Degree exam to try to prove that I could do it. I had no right to do so and was told later by Col. Butchart, the University Secretary, that I should return the Certificate, but I didn't: it was too precious to me! I have it yet!

These were two landmarks in my career; that I, an ignora-

mus, could take an English Prelim after two or three months'
study, and then pass an English Degree exam. These successes did something for my ego which I consider I needed
then. They were certainly a great boost, and I believe the Lord
used them greatly to encourage me.

To proceed to my second year in Arts I find it hard to be
precise about events since my diaries unfortunately only go
back to 1943. It was during that year, however, that I met one
with whom my Christian life and service have been closely
bound up ever since, James Philip. At the same time I
continued my connection with the Christian Students' Fellowship and formed a large circle of Christian friends.

Moral Philosophy was taught at that time by the formidable John Laird who was determined that we would not stray
too far into the subject of religion. This I found exceedingly
hard since I knew that the ethical commandments of the
second Table of the Mosaic Law stood and were built upon the
commands of the first Table, the Godward ones. The value
of the class was that it helped one to think abstractly and to
clarify one's notions on many things. But one always
gravitated towards the subject which was the reason for being
at University, and I did not care very much for the subject of
Moral Philosophy for its own sake, which means I suppose
that I was not likely to be much of a moral philosopher like
my friends James Wernham and John Wilson, both of whom
proceeded to take Advanced courses on the subject, with
logic. My lack of rational thought to which I referred earlier
perhaps mitigated against me in this respect.

I should say that James Wernham was the younger brother
of Archie who had been a phenomenon at Gordon's College
and University, and later became Professor of Moral Philosophy at Aberdeen. He married, incidentally, a young lady who
on War Service acted as a bus conductress on the route

between Broad Street and Old Aberdeen.

The subject of Psychology I found somewhat more to my liking, although again there was so much that was academic and detailed in relation to man's physical powers and susceptibilities to sight and sound that one got bogged down in all sorts of researches into what one thought and felt. However, there is no doubt that the subject afforded the beginnings of an understanding of human psychology which has been for me an inestimable gain in understanding my own human nature, and that of those whom I was called to serve and care for.

All sorts of minor skills were called for in the varied work of the Psychology class, and one day when seated next to a tall young man of friendly mien I discovered that we were expected to do a little mathematics. Having left school at the stage when we were only doing decimals, I was completely lost. I nudged him and appealed for help - after all, he was one of the bright boys who had come up from Gordon's College, an athlete as well as a scholar. So James Philip helped me. I think we walked out of class together that day. I had seen him at King's during my first year and saw that he belonged to the circle of Gordon's College boys (I had been there for a fortnight when I was 13!) but had had no occasion to speak with him.

James and I discovered almost at once that we were both interested in music - he was a singer, and played the piano - and I later learned that he belonged to Bucksburn and went to Dr. Morrison's Church. His mother had been in The Salvation Army at John Street where I had often played my brass instrument in boyhood, and the piano later on.

James' aunts, his father's sisters, who lived with the family, went to the Gordon Mission, and both he and his younger brother George, had some connection with that

Mission, its people and its work.

It was, I think after one of our Psychology classes one day that James Philip having left the bus at Bucksburn, was knocked down, and was carried I think, unconscious, to his home nearby. Hearing about this, I went to the library at Marischal College to retrieve James' lecture notes, which had been gathered from the street, and took them to his home. That was my first meeting with his family: he was still in bed but recovering. And so began a precious friendship in which we have been associated in the Lord's work ever since.

History was one of the subjects of the three I took in my second year in Arts. I enjoyed it most. The rule at King's in those days was that two historical periods alternated, year by year for first year History students: one year the Reformation period was studied, the next the period of the French Revolution. Fortunately for me, the period that year was the Reformation, so that I was given a historical background to some of the theological studies I would be launched into in Divinity the following year.

I don't know that I did very well in my History class exams, but I worked very hard at my essays, and while the class exam marks cannot have been bad (since I turned out to be first equal in a Class of 80), I see that in five essays over the year I have an alpha for four, and beta double plus for the other. The commendatory remarks by the examiner at the end of these were encouraging, and when the marks for the year's work came out, Professor Cameron of Greek stopped me in the Quadrangle and commented favourably on my results. Doubtless knowing how poorly I had done in my unequal struggle with classical Greek the year before, he was surprised.

Perhaps I was not such a numskull after all, although I knew that my difficulties were not only due to my lack of secondary education, but also to the fact that I did not have a studious mind of the academic sort, and was perhaps more romantic than systematic in outlook, with an intuitive more than a logical mind. So much for my academic studies that year.

It must have been in February of that year (1941) that I became President of the Christian Student's Fellowship. However, I soon began to find the rather narrow outlook of the pietistic members somewhat claustrophobic, especially since by then I was making friends with a wider circle of students, both church-minded and not. I ended my exasperation by resigning from the C.S.F. and because the Student Christian Movement was at a rather low ebb on account of the War situation, I was soon appointed President of that body. That only lasted a month or two because I was soon peppered with literature, advice and instructions from Professor Donald Baillie of St. Andrews University. It seemed that the trend of things in that movement was going against my grain being rather too churchy and intellectual, and I resigned from that position also the same year! It was attendance at an S.C.M. Conference at St. Andrews that put me off. It was a desolating experience: the air of cold, intellectual churchianity was so very different from the simple devoutness and evangelistic zeal of the C.S.F. So it was as a result of dissociating myself from both societies that in long earnest discussion with sympathetic contemporaries we began to formulate new plans for Christian witness, especially at King's. If I remember rightly these plans only came to fruition in the autumn of 1941 when I entered my first year in Divinity.

* * * * * *

Things were happening in the family that year. My elder brother John had been married to Reta Leiper in August 1931. By March '41 my younger brother David was also married.

He married Ethel Sang just prior to departing for the Middle
East and wore his RAF uniform for the occasion. Three
months later Ellie, my second sister, married Edwin Dewar.
At all the above ceremonies I played the organ, even playing
again on the Salvation Army Citadel's organ for Ellie's
wedding. Finally, in March '42 Rene married. She was my
youngest sister and I was her fiancee, Norman Heath's, best
man. This time my new friend, James Philip took my place at
the organ.

* * * * * *

Back to summer 1941. I can't remember when I resigned as
organist of the Gallowgate Church but it must have been some
time over that summer or into the autumn before I embarked
on my Divinity studies, for then I was soon plunged into
sustained work in a pastoral capacity with other congregations. But before leaving the subject of Gallowgate I must say
that I learned a lot from Archie Inglis and became firm friends
with his wife and daughter, Marie. There was a lively fellowship at Gallowgate amongst whom were the remnants of a
Mission church which under the Rev. Mr. Livingstone, who
later became minister at Skene, used to hold drunks-raids at
the closing of the public houses in that wild area on Saturday
evenings - shades of my Salvation Army experience!

A new generation had arisen in the Gallowgate after that,
who knew little of aggressive evangelism, but there was still
an air of the truly evangelical about the congregation (as a
Mission church it had been under the wing of Beechgrove
Church) and I suppose I felt more at home there after my Army
experience than I would have done in any church in town,
with the possible exception of Torry United Free. It is
interesting that one of the most spiritual elders at Gallowgate
was Mr. Stephen who was also Sunday School Superintend-

ent, and of course I taught in Sunday School while I was there. I became very friendly with Mrs. Stephen who belonged to Peterhead and knew vaguely some of my father's relatives in Buchanhaven.

The Stephen's daughter, Isabel (Sibi) was an active worker in the church and played the piano for the Sunday School. I can't remember when it happened but during my sojourn at Gallowgate my student friend Alex Crockett must have come to church and met Sibi, from which ensued their romance, courtship and marriage and a long friendship between the three of us. Indeed, their elder daughter Isabel returned to Aberdeen to study, when we became firm friends; she married a Christian doctor, Michael Fisher, and they served for a time at the hospital at Nazareth although at the time of writing Michael is a General Practitioner at Southampton. Alex and Sibi's elder son, Stewart, used to worship regularly with us when he was free from his work of helicopter maintenance at Dyce.

CHAPTER 7

STUDENT DAYS

During the summer of 1941 because of my dissatisfaction with both Christian Unions (C.S.F. and S.C.M.) and because a rather mixed group of students were also seeking for something new, we began to discuss the possibility of a new venture of Christian witness at King's College.

It must have been about that time that I was playing the organ at King's College Chapel Morning Prayers from 8.45 to 9 a.m. They were taken mostly by our Church History teacher, Professor G. D. Henderson and Professor James Robertson, our New Testament teacher, both of whom lived nearby. Only a handful attended, sometimes no more than three or four, which made singing difficult.

By this time the University's annual *Religions and Life Week* was becoming dry and dull, and some of us students (John Lee and John Wilson were contemporary with me, John Watt entered Divinity the next year, and Betty Sangster whom I'd got to know through S.C.M., and whose father was the devout Session Clerk of St. Nicholas Union Grove Church) all got together and spent many hours pondering what we could do to liven things up spiritually at King's.

Two things were devised. The first was an Annual Chapel Week, when interesting and arresting speakers would address the students for twenty minutes in Chapel in the context of a service of worship with hearty singing and a musical item (for

example Eileen Watt singing Mozart's Alleluia, or Kitty
Benson playing the slow movement from Max Bruch's Violin
Concerto, etc.). This continued for five days and the Chapel
was packed, some Professors even allowing students to miss
lectures to attend. Professor Noble of the Chair of Humanity
(Latin) was particularly enthusiastic and encouraged us all he
could. We often met him while fire-watching at night at
Elphinstone Hall, which we did in case of incendiary bombs:
we had many chats with him on religious and spiritual issues.

Our other venture was to suggest to the Divinity authorities
that Morning Prayers at 8.45 a.m. should cease, and instead
we should have a short service in the Chapel between 10 a.m.
and 11 a.m. lectures, lasting from 10.56 to 11.3 precisely. It
took us days of discussion to find a name for this service but
eventually, on the analogy of Evensong, called it Morningsong and it took place five days a week. At first it was
conducted by ourselves, and then by other interested students.
The short service consisted of a few verses of a hymn, a
reading, and a prayer, with an organ voluntary before and
after. It was amazing how accommodating everyone was,
even William Swainson, the organist, and this venture, soon
launched, continued for probably something like 40 years,
only ceasing several years ago. In our day the Chapel was
seldom less than packed and it was great to see the students
crowding in and taking an interest in what was done, including
the voluntaries.

It happened, therefore, that by 1942 I had ceased to hold
office in either the Christian Students' Fellowship or the
Student Christian Movement, and I concentrated my University efforts on the witness at King's College. Many hours
were spent in the quietness of the Chapel (to which we were
kindly given access) discussing spiritual things with fellow-
students: the building became a haven and spiritual home for

many in those days, and I cannot enter it now without floods
of memories.

One thing we did miss was the gorgeous Strachan windows
in the Chapel, amongst the most beautiful one can see, and so
valued that they were removed during the War and stored,
because King's College Chapel was the first target German
bombers would see on crossing the coast. In fact, I never saw
the beauty of these windows until I returned to conduct
weddings years afterwards, their glorious blues and purples
providing such a symphony of colour that there used to be a
rule about weddings in the Chapel that only white flowers
were permitted. Indeed, the present Minister of the Mither
Kirk of St. Nicholas, my friend James Stewart, was saying
only recently that during the Central Churches Holy Week
Services in Gilcomston he was greatly blessed simply looking
at our Ascension window, which is also by Strachan, (as are
Faith, Hope and Charity - curiously enough Charity is the
smallest of the three) above our West doorway.

* * * * * *

During my University career, I was engaged over periods of
some months with four particular churches, although I had
found it hard to determine in the absence of one or two diaries
which order I served them in. It was, however, St. Paul's,
Rosemount first, where I became involved during my first
year in Divinity towards the end of 1941. I can't remember
how that came about except that I had a number of contacts
with St. Paul's people. Indeed, my cousin, Hilda Steven had
been Primary Leader there for many years, and I also knew
some of the students from that congregation, including Scott
Couper, George Sangster, later of Queen's Cross Church,
and Ian Forbes, now the retired minister of Kemnay. I had a
happy seven months there preaching twice a Sunday and

getting to know the Interim Moderator, Mr. McCulloch from Bon-Accord Church across the road. I also worked with George Youngson, the organist, with whom I had much in common. At the end of that stint, about the time when I was finishing my first year in Divinity, May 1942, I was presented by the St. Paul's people with a series of volumes of the *International Critical Commentary* - the Four Gospels, I and II Corinthians, and Ephesians.

My next assignment which I think must have begun that summer, was to St. Mary's Pittodrie. My connection with St. Mary's was through the Gallowgate congregation which I had joined as organist following my final departure from the Army. Their church, it transpired, had sadly been bombed. Looking for a new building, the homeless Gallowgate people had been invited to join St. Mary's. St. Mary's therefore became a union of three churches: the remnants of the old St. Mary's Church in High Street, Old Aberdeen (now the Psychology Department of the University), the Congregational Church which devoted Ian MacAlister had gathered from their New Seaton housing estate and which formerly worshipped in a wooden hut at Pittodrie, and the Gallowgate congregation. It was not an easy union with its three strands, and the simple Seaton folk in particular were rather over-awed by the grand 'cathedral' which was built for them on King Street opposite the University Playing Fields. But it was a happy thought to have my old Gallowgate friends with me since they still had some very devoted members.

Soon after the three elements of the congregation were joined and there was a vacancy, I was asked about mid-1942, if I would act as preacher and attend to such pastoral work as was within my province and look after the Youth Organisations. I was ably supported by my dear friend John Lee, although he had Sunday commitments elsewhere. He helped

with the Youth organisations and I ran the Sunday School.
Since the Gallowgate Kirk had, like many Eastend Churches,
a pastoral connection with a Westend Church, in this case
Beechgrove, one or two members of Beechgrove acted as
teachers, of whom one was faithful Miss Taylor, who is still
my neighbour in Beaconsfield Place.

This piece of service at Pittodrie gave me great satisfaction, and I was encouraged in the work by Professor John
Graham who lived in Old Aberdeen and came along occasionally to the services with Mrs. Graham. Also some of the
notable members of Beechgrove came along on a Sunday
evening, and I recall that one such evening when I was
speaking on the peace of God as I had known it, a lecturer from
the Teacher Training College brought along a colleague who
was on the verge of a breakdown, and the word went to his
heart. His friend came to tell me how much that message
meant to him which was a great encouragement to me. This
was the first indication that the experience of my own earlier
throes would prove profitable. My service ended at Pittodrie
in December 1942 when the Sunday School presented me
with a further volume of the *International Critical Commentary*, the Book of Job, and the Boys' Brigade with a modern
translation of the New Testament inscribed with the names
of the officers and boys. I have happy memories of the people
there and of the work: during my days at Pittodrie I think I
must have visited practically every house on the Seaton estate.

* * * * * *

I was now in my second year of Divinity, and the next request
was, surprisingly enough, from Gilcomston Park Baptist
Church, during their vacancy on the departure of a minister
whose liberal views had shocked that pious people accustomed to dear old Grant Gibb. It was during my ministry there

that the Deacons asked if I would conduct the simple Communion always held at the close of the morning service, and although I had had little to do with Communion services since I had first been initiated into the Lord's Supper as organist of Crown Terrace Methodist Church, I agreed. One day I confided to Denny Grieve, my contemporary in Divinity, and son of MacKenzie Grieve of John Knox, Gerrard Street, that I was taking this simple Communion Service. This he duly reported, so that I was soon up before the Convener of the Presbytery's Committee in charge of Divinity Students. The Convener, Roderick Bethune of Beechgrove Church, told me that if I did not cease taking this communion service, being unordained, I would no longer be a candidate for the Church of Scotland ministry. Thereafter, while I preached, I simply had to sit and let the Deacons take the Breaking of Bread.

It was a privilege to minister at Gilcomston Park, not least because of the wonderful tradition of missionary service of their members of an earlier day. There was a large composite picture hung in the church hall full of inset photographs of those who had served and were serving in various mission fields. During that time there was some severe bombing in Aberdeen, including the part destruction of Causewayend Church, and houses opposite. Amongst the dead was a Deacon of Gilcomston Park Church belonging to a faithful family, and I had to take the funeral service. It was one of my first experiences of dealing pastorally with that degree of tragedy.

I recall that it was during that period that I was singing in the University Choir, and at a Sunday afternoon recital in the Cowdray Hall I was to play the organ, mostly filling in orchestral parts. I had also some piano work to do. I think it was then that I realised that I was not made of the stuff that would make a professional musician. It took too much out of me and at such performances I did not always have the presence of mind necessary for absolute precision - an amateur I really was and by then was glad to remain so, since I had found my real vocation. I remember that Sunday evening hurrying to Gilcomston Park and thinking how much better it was to go to church than to a concert hall!

While I was at Gilcomston Park it was suggested that I might organise a sacred music recital and ask some of my musical friends from the University to join me. That took place on Thursday June 24th, with Eileen Watt, Soprano, Janet Ogilvie, Contralto, Kathleen Benson, Violin, and myself at the Roger's Grand Piano installed for the occasion: I have the programme yet.

Eileen sang Mozart's 'Allelulia', 'With Verdure Clad' from Haydn's Creation, and 'My Heart ever Faithful' by Bach. Janet sang 'He was despised' from Messiah, 'Legend' by Tschaikovsky, and Negro spirituals. She also sang 'He hath filled the Hungry' by Bach, and 'God shall wipe away all Tears' by Sullivan. Kathleen played the Adagio from Bruch's Violin Concerto, Sonata No. 4 by Handel, and the Andante, Allegretto and Allegro from Mendelsshon's Violin Concerto. I played 'Subdue us by Thy Goodness' by Bach, Beethoven's Moonlight Sonata, the Chromatic Fantasia by Bach, 'To the Spring' by Grieg, Nocturne in B. Major by Chopin, and 'Island Spell' by John Ireland. The Recital, which was in aid of Church funds came to an end with Eileen and Janet singing 'He shall feed His Flock', and 'Come Unto Him' from Messiah.

The Recital was a new venture, although we had been doing this sort of thing at King's College Chapel. It pleased people greatly, and because during the war there was so little diversion or relief from stress and strain, people crowded to such an occasion. (It was this, later on in August 1945 that gathered crowds into Gilcomston in the early hours of the morning following the cessation of the War in the Far East. And it was this spirit that gave the first days of the ministry in Gilcomston its impetus.)

The St. Paul's people next door knowing of this Recital would not be left out, and although I was no longer with them, since their new Minister, Thomas Crawford had arrived in October of that year (my last year in Divinity), I undertook a Recital in St. Paul's with the same three helpers, and with me at the organ. Another programme was arranged for that occasion with too many items to enumerate here, but I have a copy of it. It took place on Sunday afternoon 24th October, 1943.

The news of these recitals went round, and I was asked to take part in a Recital in the Grammar School Hall with Eileen Watt and Kathleen Benson at the request of a teacher there, Charles Forbes who sang art songs beautifully. I was solo pianist and Mrs. Forbes played the accompaniments. I envied her because I felt I was more suited to the accompanist's rather than the soloist's role. I was only too aware that attention would be focused on me and it was a considerable strain to one who was beginning to feel, increasingly, that music was not really his line. Although I loved it, mine was to be another profession.

* * * * * *

That autumn, I was invited to become student Assistant at John Knox's Church, Mounthooly, and it was during that winter that the suggestion was made that I might co-operate with other musicians in the annual Students' Theatre Show. I had certain misgivings about this so near to my licensing as a preacher of the Gospel, but I had such a circle of friends at University and they were so keen that I should do it and perhaps lift the tone of the show somewhat, that I agreed. Not every musical person in the University was pleased. 'Oh,' it was said, 'he'll give us Bach!' What they did not know was that I had been friendly with a young cripple student doing English Literature who had written an operetta and wanted someone to set it to music. I said I would try, and so 'The Royal Rebel', an old world affair with eighteenth century costumes and a pastiche on Gilbert and Sullivan was the result. It ended the first half of the show.

But the piece that ended the show was a visionary set of tableaux called 'And I Saw', which James Duncan, later minister of King Street Church, and who died in harness due to trouble contracted in the war, culled from the book of Revelation. The tableaux were meant to present what the different faculties of the University could contribute to the new world which was so earnestly looked for at the end of the war. We saw medics and scientists and cadets and scholars at work in their various departments, and all accompanied with music which it was my task to compose. I think Beethoven was my main inspiration for this, as Sullivan was for the operetta, and I sought to use a dignified restraint which the critics thought was effective. Certainly the effect with the scenes on the stage and these solemn chords was impressive. It ended with the whole cast of the show dressed in their red togas, singing Gaudeamus, the universal students' anthem. We sang three verses of it in different keys and with differing vocal arrangements with the last verse set in six-part harmony. I believe God gave me some particular chords towards the climax of the finale and I revelled in it. I was able many years later on my seventieth birthday to recall some of that music on the organ at Gilcomston, but it was not the same as with a chorus of about sixty young student voices singing their hearts out.

The six months' winter service at John Knox's with the Rev. T. Maxwell McAuslane were happy times and I made many friends in that old parish church congregation. It was there that being exasperated by the unwillingness of local churches and their ministers to help some of us Christian students to do something for the young people parading Union Street in the black-out, especially on Saturday and Sunday evenings, I preached a sermon at the 3 p.m. afternoon service in John Knox's in which I hit out at their non-co-operation, and immediately sent a copy of my script to the local Press. It appeared in the Evening Express under the bold headline DIVINITY STUDENT CRITIC OF CHURCH. Within a few days I was again before the Rev. Roderick Bethune for insubordination and was warned not to say such things again, especially so near my licensing as a preacher, which could come into question.

We gave two recitals in John Knox's Church that winter. One on Sunday 30th January, at 3 p.m. when Muriel Maitland and Duncan Murray both belonging to John Knox's helped Eileen Watt and Kit Benson and me in a programme which included music by Bach, Handel, Haydn, Mozart, Mendelssohn, Gounod, Rachmaninoff, Elgar and Sullivan. On the back page of the programme I made an attempt at verse, but all that a classical student friend would say about it was that the thoughts had been better expressed. But he did not say by whom! I would have sought to learn from him. Here it is:

All ye who enter now
This temple of the Lord Most High
Where countless hearts have sought and found
eternal peace and fortitude
lay by the stress and strain of hectic days
of fevered rush and unfilled longing

refuse the memory of a thousand pains and irks
that would inflame the soul
And lead to its distemper
And let the pure sweet music of the ages
Distil its essence of celestial sound
And waft our spirits to ethereal bounds
Where peace and love and joy are found
To merge in one sonorous paean
Of joyful psalm and symphony.
And if perchance there linger still
In some dark cavern of the soul's abode
One dreadful thought of pride
Of guile or folly, lust or hate
Then Christ is here in holy love
To purge the heart and tune it in
To hear the mystic harmony
That echoes down the timeless halls
Of God's unspann'd eternity.
O restless spirit yield to Him
Confess whilst that unspoken urge
Implores you to lay bare to Him
The secrets of your soul's intent
Confessing which the veil is rent
Which hides the sinner from his God
And God and you will meet today
And bells shall peal and organs play
And harps and trumps and voices blend
To fill the world with ecstasy
For that a soul has found at last
The key, the tune, the rhythm free
Of holy heavenly harmony.

The second recital took the place of the Sunday evening service on April 16th, the time of year allowing our meeting without the church being blacked-out. Charles Forbes helped Eileen Watt, Muriel Maitland, Kit Benson and me in another programme of suitable Sunday evening music, concluding with a short address by the Minister, Mr. McAuslane, who had been a real friend to me. That was the conclusion of a week which had involved me in conducting the theatre show for six evenings, with my licensing in the West Church of St. Andrew on the Tuesday evening (Andrew Shivas conducting the finale of the first act, the operetta, in my absence), and attending the students' ball on Thursday evening in the Music Hall, where I was asked to accompany Mamie Cant in one of the numbers from the Royal Rebel with the cast present joining in. On Wednesday morning after the licensing, while one or two of the young ministers threatened to parade Union Street with their clerical collars, John Lee, John Wilson and I determined that instead we would row up the river Dee in a boat, which we did.

* * * * * *

Now, I have to say that although I tried to carry out all these musical programmes, since it represented different sides of my life then, underneath I was far from easy. As I hurried from the West Church of St. Andrew that Tuesday evening after my licensing with my presentation Bible under my arm and hastened to the stage door of His Majesty's, I hoped no one would see me and know what I was doing. I did meet that week, Helen Smith in Union Terrace and she tackled me about my theatrical career in the midst of what was regarded as the most sacred time of my life thus far. I, of course, passed it off. What could one do? However, I have to say this, that while my colleagues in Divinity were taking that service very

seriously, regarding it as the Lord's seal on their call to the
ministry, I could say, despite my escapade, that the Lord had
laid his hand on me for service long years before that, in the
midst of my throes of ill-health. So that, stray a little, I might,
but nothing could deter me from fulfilling my calling: I had
come to it at too great a cost. However, as I am about to relate,
the plaudits of my friends and the local Press music critic
George Rowntree Harvey unnerved me a little, and when I
thought of Springburn, in Glasgow where I was engaged to
work for a year as an assistant, and all the depressing tenement
stairs that I was about to mount in the interest of the Lord's
work, I shuddered.

There is, however, one experience of that time which must
be related. The music for the theatre show was conceived in
all sorts of places and times, even sitting at my final lectures,
and standing in a queue for tickets for that very show. I remember scribbling out merry little tunes in what I thought was
the style of Sullivan, leaning against the wall at His Majesty's.
The writing out of band parts, after the huge undertaking of
writing the vocal parts for the cast and chorus was a killing
task. That had been done earlier and rehearsals were almost
completed except that we had not performed in the actual
theatre with the theatre orchestra.

By the Friday before the orchestra rehearsal, many of the
parts were not complete. That Friday was as usual Fire-
watching night at Woolmanhill, and so after tea at six o'clock
I went to a place apart and began to work on them. Bed-time
came, and there was still much to do, but what could I do but
continue, and I did, until the morning. I remember the cleaner
coming into the room where I was and saying, 'O, you're up
early!' And I simply said, 'Yes.' But it was done. But then,
to hear how it sounded. After a few snags it sounded all right,
and when the whole thing was taken together I was astonished

that it could come out as it did. Vast relief! That was my first
attempt at conducting a professional orchestra, and playing
my own music. It was my last, too. Nor am I sorry. It closed
my musical career. Yet it was not an easy renunciation.

I had been with the officials of the Theatre show at dinner
in the Athenaeum on the Thursday before the performance,
with the ball afterwards in the Music Hall. I was back again
in the Athenaeum on the following Monday for lunch with
George Rowntree Harvey the local critic of music and drama,
himself a dramatist of no mean worth (witness his play on
Elphinstone concerning the beginnings of Aberdeen University). He knew that I was about to leave for Springburn for
an Assistant Minister's post there, and he kindly deplored that
I had chosen the wrong career! I think it was the symphonic
nature of that Gaudeamus that took him, as well as the lilting
melodies of the operetta, but I attributed the one to Beethoven
- bless him, and the other to Sullivan. However, I was
flattered, and it was in the end with a rather heavy heart that
I contemplated the tenements of Springburn!

CHAPTER 8

GLASGOW

Next Sunday, 23rd April, I preached my last sermon at John Knox's where the people had been remarkably responsive, and the next week-end, near my thirty-third birthday on 8th May, I set out on my own to look at Springburn and Springburnhill Parish Church: 'the Kirk on the hill' or the 'Hill Kirk' they called it, which was an extension from Glasgow Cathedral. Alas, on the Saturday I found the manse closed, and next morning at Church I learned that the new minister, the Rev. William Fitch who was to be my 'Bishop' had gone on a short holiday. I gained little impression, therefore, of what life would be like in that environment with an avowedly evangelical man coming to an old parish church. Bill Fitch, was one of three minister brothers and two doctors, (his only sister, Mary married Arthur Wallace, an Aberdonian, a brother of James Wallace, one time minister at Gardenstown). Bill had been minister of Newmilns in Ayrshire, the Church from which Tom Allan came, and in which Roderick Bethune had been minister. I recall meeting Tom Allan later, actually, in Bill Fitch's bedroom. Bill had been unwell and Tom Allan, still in the uniform of an RAF pilot, was visiting him before being demobilised.

A few weeks after my rather fruitless visit to spy out the land at the Hill Kirk, I was back as assistant, having found temporary lodgings. But I had an idea of where to find more permanent lodgings: I had learned that a former music pupil of mine, Kate Pirie whom I had sought to teach organ at Monymusk Parish Church, where she played, had moved from their farm of Elrick near Alford in Aberdeenshire to Glasgow, and had bought 7, Park Terrace, and had called it the Bon-Accord Hotel. They were delighted to have me, and although the area of Kelvingrove Park which the Terrace overlooked was rather far from Springburn, there was a direct tram service from Charing Cross to two possible locations in Springburn.

I remained with the Piries for the duration of my stay in Glasgow, and was witness to many exciting events there, including a visit for a night of Sir Thomas Mitchell, former Lord Provost of Aberdeen who had been stranded in Glasgow after a meeting. He knew my father through a mutual business associate, William Watt Hepburn, who became the local millionaire tycoon, but who was brought up in Gardenstown along with my father. My father used to say Watt Hepburn started business as a boy breeding and selling rabbits! Bon-Accord Hotel had been the home of the wealthy Reid family of one of the great railway locomotive yards in Springburn, almost the home of that kind of transport. It was a palatial place, with marble staircases and bathrooms, with beautiful carved balustrades and huge rooms of perfect proportions. I had a small dressing-room which was easy to heat, and suited me well.

The year in Glasgow was in some ways definitive for me. There is no doubt that I had slipped somewhat from my evangelical faith during my divinity years. It was not only the critical and liberal nature of the studies applied to the Scriptures and the Church that caused my intellectual and spiritual conflict and seemed to shake my beliefs; there was also the fact that during war time in the University, considerably

reduced in every way as it was, I had become something of a
character, and my popularity had grown throughout my five
years there, with the climax of my final year, as I have
described. To get down to hard graft after being something
of a local celebrity and with my faith somewhat eroded I found
it irksome, especially when faced with a young evangelical
minister, scholar though he was, having just completed a PhD.
on Kierkegaard, the Danish existential theologian. He was a
true pietist and the product of the United Free Church which
had rejoined the Church of Scotland in 1929, and also of the
Mission Hall, Falkirk where his father was, I believe, the
redoubtable superintendent.

I soon reacted against Bill Fitch's determination to make
a deep impression upon that typical parish church congregation. I must admit I worked very hard at systematic visitation
of the congregation, and with an excellent index system I
think I must have visited most of the congregation of something like 1,500 members in the months I was active there,
from June to the end of November. But I was tugging at Bill
Fitch's rather dogmatic style, with regard to what he would
allow, and what he would not allow in the congregational set-
up. Deeper than that, I was not at ease spiritually at all in this
determinedly evangelical environment - until an argument
with a train in Troon railway station brought me to my senses
at last!

I had been asked to speak at the Woman's Guild of St.
Meddan's Church, Troon, where Bill Fitch's older brother,
Tom was minister. I stayed the night and while waiting for the
Glasgow train to arrive a few steps from the manse, I chatted
with Mrs. Fitch. I delayed too long, with the result that I
reached the platform and rushed forward to open a carriage
door just as the train started and accelerated with a speed
which still astonishes me as I think of it. It pulled me along,

and I began to feel myself being sucked down between the platform and the track. I had to let go, but received such a jolt on doing so that I fell onto the platform, my foot aching, and was not able to get up. Taken back to the manse to await a later train I was practically carried into it and was assured that Bill Fitch would be meeting me at Glasgow. He was, and took me right away to a specialist, who X-rayed my ankle and pronounced it badly broken. I would have to go to the Western Infirmary, and there in Ward 32 I remained throughout December, January and half of February. It was a humiliating and yet a refining experience.

The ankle was badly broken, and would have to be pinned, then plastered, but the wound became badly infected. A window was cut out at the point of the wound, and I was taken periodically to the theatre to have it dressed. At one point, although I didn't know it until later, there was word of possibly amputating the foot. I was told by Mr. Hutton, the chief surgeon, that I could come back in a year and have the steel pin removed. I never did, and have it yet, and when, upon a less serious injury to that ankle I was X-rayed in Aberdeen, they wanted to know what this was in my ankle: it had practically become part of my foot, and there it will stay, until the foot crumbles away!

I was therefore out of the battle at Springburnhill not only during these months in hospital but until mid-April, when my leg became sufficiently strong for me to contemplate returning to Glasgow from Aberdeen, to try to resume my duties until the end of my year.

I recall that there was a controversy with the Treasurer of the Hill Kirk because I wanted to decline my salary these months, and he, Mr. McLaughlan, a gracious business man who had been a Glasgow town councillor, insisted that it was my right. It was the only way I could show how grieved I was at letting Bill Fitch and the Church down. He would have had to run that huge Church on his own for these nearly five months, but fortunately there was a divinity student around, from Lewis I think, who took on my duties for the duration, whose name was Alex John (and I can't remember his surname, it may have been MacLeod) who later became minister of Portree, Skye.

* * * * * *

During these long days in hospital, my mind drifted and switched from one possibility for my future to another. At times I despaired, thinking that, considering my unfortunate career health-wise before, and the mess I had made of my assistantship, working hard but not being on too cordial terms with William Fitch, I was a bit of a failure, and if any remote place would be willing to have me, I would have to be content with that. I remember that the parish of Durness, near Cape Wrath was for a long time vacant then, and I wondered if I might get that! In later years John Moir, one of our divinity boys at Gilcomston went there to preach for a summer, and I recalled the earlier thought I had had in hospital. These months were undoubtedly times of refinement, and I resolved that if and when I had the chance, I would be a true minister of God's Word, and shed the critical notions I had acquired during my training.

I must record here my profound gratitude to my landlady, Kate Pirie who, busy as she was with her hotel, came regularly to visit me at the Western Infirmary and brought gifts. The Fitches from Troon and their friends, the Roberts also came, as did an exceedingly devout Nazarene pastor, Mr. McLaggan (whose son at the time of writing is Church of Scotland minister in Largs). That dear man brought a breath of God to my little side-room, and I could believe it was possibly after he had prayed with me and for me, that my mind clarified and my heart was at rest, and I determined that I would simply be the Lord's servant, wherever he took me. My brother John came to see me from Aberdeen, as on another occasion, my sister Barbara.

Lyra Henderson, the jeweller David Henderson's wife, also came one day to visit me from Largs (they had a hotel there), with a bag of huge Jaffa oranges. Mrs. Henderson had brought a specific message. David had worked during the war at the Aberdeen Food Office, where Walker Leith the Treasurer of Gilcomston also worked, and they had become friends. Walker had engaged David's interest in the plight of Gilcomston South, and had actually organised a garden party at his house in Bieldside, which was opened by Tom Taylor, of the Chair of Law at the University and later its Principal. The deficit, which prevented the Presbytery giving Gilcomston the right to call a minister was wiped out, and the go ahead given. Hence Mrs. Henderson's visit. Would I be interested? I told her that my teacher, Professor G. D. Henderson had said that no man should consider ministering in his home town, but was better to find a place otherwise. But I also said that I wanted to remain in the big city, Glasgow - which was rather different from wondering whether even remote Durness would have me! - such are the fluctuations of the mind of those who speculate on the place of their calling. I think Mrs. Henderson went away somewhat daunted, but looking back I'm sure that I was very definite that I was not coming back to Aberdeen, and to that Church!

From the time of my return home to Aberdeen on the 15th February, 1945 I waited until the ankle grew stronger. I was still on crutches, then on two sticks, then one, and I recall that the first time I ventured beyond home without any support, I was very nervous. It was my brother-in-law, Norman Heath,

in Aberdeen then, following his demobilisation from the army
having suffered a fearful accident which disfigured his face,
who said to me, 'Throw away your stick, man!' I did. But
that was later. On my return home, Erskine Blackburn of
Holburn Central Church, who had taken over the Interim
Moderatorship of Gilcomston South from Rev. W. W. Gauld
of Queen's Cross (he who hoped that when Gilcomston
became defunct, its beautiful carved oak could be transferred
to Queen's Cross Church whose wood was not so fine!) came
to call on me and presented the need of the vacant Gilcomston,
and pleaded with me to consider it. At that time it did not occur
to me why they were all so keen for me to take Gilcomston.
They had already advertised for a minister and had received
twenty-seven applications, including one from a man who
later came to Christ's College as an academic. They rejected
them all, and determined to try again, since the man who came
would need to have something about him to pull the Church
out of its slough of despond.

It had been Walker Leith's idea to have me. We had never
met, but he had heard of our music recitals in town, and that
great crowds had been gathered for them. He thought, 'If I can
get that man, he will draw a crowd.' He later told me that he
did not care whether I brought a brass band into his beloved
Church as long as I filled it! However, I said the same to
Erskine Blackburn as I had said to Mrs. Henderson in hospital
in Glasgow - No, and told him what G. D. Henderson had said
about trying to minister in one's home town, especially since
I had been popular as a student figure in town.

CHAPTER 9

BACK TO ABERDEEN

The weeks passed as I waited to be mobile enough to return to Springburn, and one Sunday evening I said to my Aunt Bella who, having been widowed of her fisherman husband, John Alexander, was staying with us at 31 Woodstock Road, 'Let's go to West Church of St. Andrew's and hear R. T. Cameron.' He was having informal evening services at which he did not robe but took the service from the Communion Table - a daring innovation for so prestigious a congregation. After the service, Mr. Cameron met people in the aisles, and asked me, seeing my two sticks, how I was getting on. I told him that Erskine Blackburn had been back at me a second time asking if I would consider the vacancy in Gilcomston across the road, and Mr. Cameron said, 'Well you know, my Assistant, Denny Grieve (he who 'cliped' on me taking the Communion services at Gilcomston Park Baptist Church) is doing duty there, and he says, 'Not even a St. Paul could do anything with them.' 'Oh,' said I, and left.

I cannot remember what my thoughts or words were to my Aunt as we went home that evening: we took a tram to King's Gate, and waited there for a bus to take us up to Woodstock Road. While waiting (I could take you to the precise spot, and, curiously enough when I pass it, it never occurs to me that that was the spot of my destiny - I must make a mark, there, one day!) - my Aunt said to me, 'What was Mr. Cameron saying to you?' I told her that he was telling me Denny Grieve's estimate of the poor people of Gilcomston South (whom the redoubtable Dr. Cox, Presbytery Clerk, and author of the ecclesiastics' bible, *Practice and Procedure in the Church of Scotland* had tried to close). I included his comment that not even a St. Paul could do anything with them. Then, quite reflectively, and without any thought of decision, or destiny, I said to her, 'Perhaps less will do!' I then became sure that I was to tackle this task, and as I promised Erskine Blackburn, having agreed to consider the matter on his second visit, I phoned him to say I would.

I preached there both services on the 1st April, 1945, mounting the pulpit with my two sticks, and at the close of the evening service, it was decided by the congregation that I should be called. I met the Vacancy Committee right away, amongst whom was this seemingly formidable figure of a lady with a huge black hat, whom I later knew as Miss Hunter, and who became my very dear friend and ardent supporter - she had just been bereaved of her darling sister, 'Little Miss Hunter' and was broken-hearted.

I thereafter returned to Springburn in a few days to try to carry out my duties, handicapped though I was. My last days at Springburn were not happy. I had not fitted into William Fitch's ministry previously, and the tension was the same as before. Kind as he and Mary his wife were to me, I felt they probably thought me a bit of a failure - certainly not calculated to be much of a minister, more a musician perhaps, for I returned to Springburnhill later to play the piano. Later still I returned to Springburn for Alan Redpath's Mission in Springburn Town Hall.

When my year ended at Springburnhill, having been off practically five months, and feeling guilty and a failure and longing to be away from the place, I was glad to speed my way back to the Aberdeen which I had formerly despised as a provincial city. I travelled home from Glasgow on the eve of my 34th birthday, which was the first night of the removal of restrictions concerning the blackout following the ending of the war on the western front, 7th May. It was obvious as the evening train made its way north that people were glad to show their lights. There was excitement even on the train!

Arrangements were hurriedly being made for the beginning of the new ministry. I was called to come and look at a house in Beaconsfield Place which was for sale for £2,200. The congregation had £1,200 in the bank, the proceeds from the sale of their former manse. David Henderson and Walker Leith were the moving spirits in this, and in the hope of soon making up the difference, they offered £2,200 for 18, Beaconsfield Place, and then an added £25 to make sure of getting it, and that has been my home ever since.

My Aunt who had been left a widow and had no family, readily agreed to come and live with me, and that had the advantage of providing me with a houseful of furniture from her home in Gardenstown. And so we moved in on, I think, the 24th of May, with the Induction on 7th June, my brother David's birthday, and I preached my first sermons as minister - no one to introduce me - on Sunday 10th June, 1945.

* * * * * *

The Induction was of course memorable to me. The Sunday before, because it was Assembly time I was asked to preach at Braemar, where I stayed at Cranford with Miss Cran who had been a teacher of eurhythmics in Aberdeen, her father having been the City Chamberlain. We became firm friends. She was great friends with Sister Anne, the Deaconess at the West Kirk, the Mother Kirk of Aberdeen, and we had many comings and goings after that, for Miss Cran ultimately came

into town and was cared for by Sister Anne until she passed
away. She is buried in the St. Nicholas Churchyard near the
main avenue.

On the Wednesday, we had the Induction, and I recall my
profound feelings as I stood there, supported by the Interim
Moderator, Erskine Blackburn, answering the questions.
This meant far more to me than either my licensing, or my
Ordination in Springburnhill, when at the latter Professor
Riddell of Trinity College, Glasgow gave the charge. I had
known that the Lord had laid his hand on me for his service,
but that was in general, although I had served in various
churches in Aberdeen and then in Glasgow. This was
different. Even if I was in this place five years, which was the
minimum in ordinary circumstances one would have to
remain in a first charge, it was still a total commitment. What
it would have done to me if I had known then that it would at
the latest time of revising this script be over forty-six years,
I don't know. But I answered the Induction questions with
trembling heart, literally crying to God inwardly that he
would enable me to be faithful.

Many came to the Induction including Roderick Bethune,
the Convenor of the Students' Committee who had sought to
discipline me as a student, once for taking communion
services at Gilcomston Park Baptist Church, and once for
sending my critical sermon to the Press. He shook hands
cordially enough with me at the Induction, and remarked to
someone, perhaps a little unctuously, that although his contacts with me had not been pleasant, he wanted to come along
to show he had no hard feelings. Bless him! He was later
exceedingly kind to John Riddell who was Student Assistant
to him at North Morningside, and who became a leading
figure in Church Courts. He had begun his ministry in
Newmilns, preceding William Fitch, the home of Tom Allan,

where Eric Alexander was to exert a beneficial ministry, to be succeeded by my young friend and brother, Ian Hamilton.

The next evening, Thursday, was the Induction Social, held in the Church, with tea afterwards in the hall. Erskine Blackburn, the Interim Moderator presided graciously, and amongst those present were R. T. Cameron from across the road - I wondered what he would think of me accepting the charge after what he told me Denny Grieve said about the people. Tom Campbell from Gilcomston St. Colms also came and spoke, and in my address (when the congregation presented me with a cheque for £10 which, they said, was all they could afford), I said, we would have to make a lot more than that if the £1,000 on the manse was to be paid off! It was paid off, as I recall, in less than a year, so great were the crowds who came in the first days.

The one thing I recall saying at that Induction Social was that, viewing this beautiful church building and its high arch over the pulpit, it would be my desire to inscribe high up on its walls the two words, CHRIST CRUCIFIED. I now think that sounded too dramatic, and I could believe that some of those present may have thought it too aggressively pietistic. We never did inscribe the walls, but better than that, we have proclaimed Christ Crucified not only in justificationary terms but in sanctificationary terms, as the Victor over all the powers of evil. Perhaps that sweeping gesture, as I turned and indicated the two breasts of the wall, was more prophetic than I realised.

It is, at this point that I choose to end an incomplete story. My years at Gilcomston are best considered under a number of topics which many consider have characterised my ministry. A chronological and extremely detailed account is already provided in the four volumes of *The Gilcomston Story*.

It remains only to simply record my thanksgiving to God

for taking a life which for most of its first thirty-four years
seemed comparatively rudderless, although far from unambi-
tious, and making something of it to his glory. Surely all that
is of lasting worth in it is to his glory. By his grace he found
for me a particular, if not peculiar niche - not that since then
my life has consistently glorified him, alas, as I freely and
sorrowfully confess; but his quiet persistency has ensured that
what ever the lapses and failures, he has always seen to it that
I was guided back into his way and made to go on to fulfil
what he intended. May it continue, but more consistently, to
the end.

Part 2

Forward Into Battle

CHAPTER 10

INVOLVEMENT WITH STUDENTS

My involvement with students started, having left school at the age of thirteen due to ill-health, in my twenty-seventh year. At a private college I prepared for prelims to enter University on a Modified Course as a candidate for the Church of Scotland ministry. The course sought no degree, but after two years of Arts the full Divinity course of three years had to be completed.

Having completed these preliminary exams with great difficulty because I was still recovering from the nervous trouble which had dogged my young life and rendered me practically invalid from the age of 23 to 28, I entered Aberdeen University in October, 1939 just as the Second World War started. I was exempt from military service and also from service with the university cadets because of the state of my health.

Although deeply impressed by the lectures and lecturers in the new world of academia, I was at sea about student life, and crept about anonymously until I met students, including Alex Crockett (later Edinburgh City Engineer), who told me about the Christian Students Fellowship. From the time I attended the C.S.F. I began to feel orientated and to take part in their activities, notably prayer and their weekly meetings.

Because I was ten years older than practically all these Christian students and, for all my ill-health, had gained a good deal of knowledge of life, not least as a musician and music teacher, I was soon making my way amongst them. Yet I had a lot to learn: I had known only the Salvation Army, apart from two years spent with the Methodist Church as organist and a brief spell with the Gallowgate Church of Scotland in the same capacity.

A significant part of that learning was meeting Brethren and Free Church students at the C.S.F. and beginning to be made aware of the tension between biblical fundamental Christians and liberals: this I had never known in all my Salvation Army experience, nor really in Methodism, although at Gallowgate with Archie Inglis (who after service in the Household Cavalry became a London City missionary) I got a whiff of the great distinction between those who believed the Bible and those who advanced their own opinions on it.

I have recalled how I became involved in the leadership of the C.S.F. and became President yet at the same time was aware of my growing exasperation with the movement and what I regarded as the narrowness of some of the members. My resignation, my subsequent appointment to the presidency of the Student Christian Movement, and resignation from that post also are all indicative of my dissatisfaction and confusion at that time in the midst of differing Biblical opinions. So, as President of both and within a few months President of neither, it was obvious there was something else for me to do.

By this time I was engaged in my Divinity Studies and was aware through my organ playing at early morning prayers in the College Chapel that there was very little interest in this aspect of spiritual life in my college. The instigation both of the Annual Chapel Week and daily Morningsong which I have already described were the product of a number of us realising this and wanting to do something to quicken this flagging spiritual life at Kings. It seemed only right that we should be concentrating our efforts on reaching out to our fellow students and to use their own chapel building for this purpose.

The willingness of the Divinity faculty and a number of lecturers from other disciplines to support us vindicated our attempts at change. Students also flocked to attend Morningsong in particular. It seemed to have the broad appeal that we had longed to achieve and which my previous involvement in Christian student societies had sadly lacked.

The musical element in both the Chapel Week and Morningsong was always strong. Yet this part of the worship did not only help to enliven Kings and attract many to the services in the College Chapel, it also led to greater things in the city itself.

Indeed, it was from these contributions that a series of Sunday afternoon recitals were held in various Churches, including the capacious John Knox Mounthooly Church, and these always drew packed congregations. They were held on Sunday afternoons because the only Church in Aberdeen fully blacked out, as it happened, was Gilcomston South which I knew nothing about then. This meant that evening activities were not permissible because of lighting restrictions during hours of darkness.

It was, of course, my involvement with students during five years at Kings which stood me in good stead when, after a short year in Glasgow as Assistant Minister to the Rev. Dr. William Fitch at Springburnhill Parish Church, I returned to Aberdeen in 1945 to become Minister of Gilcomston South Church situated on the main thoroughfare, Union Street.

Those students still at University who had known me immediately supported the new work in Gilcomston, with the addition of conscripts in the Forces who at Gordon Barracks combined military training with University classes. There were some fine Christians amongst them, including Americans, and they evangelised their fellows and brought them along to the new 7.30 p.m. evangelistic services which were begun within weeks of my Induction. Some of these erstwhile students have been notable in professional and Christian service in various continents since.

By Christmas 1945 our services were drawing large crowds, especially the 7.30 evening service, and so it was arranged than on Christmas Eve we would hold a partly choral evening service with visual representation of the stable scene at Bethlehem. Following that our children's choir toured the city singing carols to a dozen aged members of our congregation, thence back for the Christmas Eve midnight service. When we returned to Church in the late evening we found a queue encircling the block waiting to get in. By the time midnight struck every aisle in the Church, the vestibule and even up the pulpit steps was crowded with worshippers, with singing which practically drowned out the organ. It was unforgettable. The next year we had to issue tickets of admission so the congregation of Gilcomston at least could be assured of a seat.

What made that occasion particularly memorable perhaps was arriving back from the visitation to prepare for the service to find Gordon Ross, our organist struggling to get any sound out of the church organ. It was the organ motor which should pump the air which was causing the problems. He could not get it to work. 'There's absolutely no sound at all,' he cried. What were we to do with so many people crowding into the church? The only thing that he could suggest was to pump the organ by hand. There are two handles inside the organ so two men, one of whom was the church officer went into the chamber behind the pulpit and began to pump. The service - and the organ playing - went off without a hitch but to see those two men when they finally emerged from those bellows! They had almost collapsed exhausted with their efforts. The noise of over a thousand voices lustily singing Christmas carols had well-nigh drowned out the organ and Gordon had needed to play at full tilt!

* * * * * *

However, within nine months of the commencement of the ministry, in March 1946 a Youth for Christ team came to Aberdeen. For two evenings they led meetings with the young Billy Graham amongst them. He was the youngest of a team of four and perhaps the least experienced amongst them yet he was the star preacher even then. On the first night I took the opening prayer and was greatly moved to see the packed congregation with so many young folk, and I enjoyed great liberty in speaking to God. I recall as I returned to my seat in the choir stalls I found myself seated next to Billy. In his generous, human way he turned and put his arm round me and whispered a startling request in my ear: 'Will you come to America?' 'Just like that?' I queried. He nodded. I can't remember exactly what I said but I indicated that I had come there only nine months before and that here I was to stay!

When he preached on the following evening it was clear that Billy Graham was a young man of powerful preaching ability. On that evening in 1946 he spoke with great clarity and authority in what we now know to be his direct, forceful style and as soon as the meeting was over he ushered the fifty or so folk, mostly young people, who had come forward into the Session room to counsel them. Standing on a chair in the corner he proceeded to indoctrinate these new followers of Christ.

Afterwards he and the team gathered James Philip, John Breeze, Willie Brown and myself into the vestry and urged us to begin a Youth for Christ meeting in Aberdeen straight away. 'We'll not leave Aberdeen until you form one,' they said. This we agreed to do and from then on until the end of 1946, Saturday evening Youth for Christ Rallies were held in Gilcomston Church, with many young folk attending including students. Many were converted to Christ at this time and some are still with us today.

With the inspiration of the coming of the Youth for Christ Team, from March to June these Saturday Rallies and the Sunday services were exceedingly vibrant with crowded congregations, and with appeals to the congregation to sit closer in the pews and to share hymn books (we had bought eight hundred copies of Redemption Songs, to cater for our seating capacity). We tried all sorts of gimmicks: a large choir of young folk; the organ and my own Bechstein piano which I had taken down to the church and, alas, retuned half a tone to match the organ which was under pitch; testimonies; solos, as well as, of course, straight from the shoulder Gospel addresses. In addition, we stretched a huge Youth for Christ banner across the front of the church (we had tried to erect it across Union Street but this had proved impossible) and sent out large numbers of young folk onto Union Street with handfuls of invitations. We even put striking notices in the local press advertising our meetings.

That was the beginning of a hectic few months. It all caused much dismay amongst some of my Presbytery colleagues. Yet there was so much happening spiritually that not even the General Assembly could have stopped the flow. Nothing so wildly evangelistic had hit Aberdeen for years and some of the faithful who had called me to Gilcomston must have wondered also what they had unleashed. They had not bargained for this! But then neither had I, yet we were swept along by the obvious purpose of God (although I am convinced that he was not responsible for all that went on!).

As news went out beyond Aberdeen of our activities and our successes correspondence began flooding in with invitations to take meetings and evangelistic campaigns in other places. By this time, my colleague in divinity, John Lee, was Minister of a Church in the mining and very socialist town of Cowdenbeath which had been ill-served by the ministry for some time. So bad had it become that the Christian Church was in ill-repute compared with Freemasonry. John asked if I would come to Cowdenbeath with a team of students in June and hold a Mission. Of course I would. So we gathered the best of our young folk amongst whom are a number of notables in Christian service today, and when we arrived learned that the whole town was agog with what was about to happen. The first thing I saw painted in huge letters on the roadway was WHO IS STILL? then, STILL IS COMING, and then nearer the centre of the town, STILL IS HERE!

We had a thrilling fortnight of it with many converted, especially some of the Y.M.C.A. boys who served the Lord faithfully to the end of their days. One night after the meeting in the Church, I was asked if I would answer questions to these young men from the Y.M.C.A. I was very willing, and so until late at night I was plied with questions when God gave me almost supernatural cogency. When the last question was answered and I had prayed with them, I went to see about locking up assuming that the others had gone home. But when I tried the vestry door it would only open an inch or two. Inside all the team were there on their knees crying to God for me. I then knew why God had given me the ability to answer the young folks' questions. That taught me more than anything about the immediacy and sufficiency of prayer.

Yet there was exhaustion after this exciting campaign although I had to return to the enthusiasm fostered in Aberdeen at this time. I did fit in a short camping holiday with my three staunchest friends, James Philip, John Breeze and Willie Brown but by October Gilcomston was involved in Alan Redpath's mission in Aberdeen's Music Hall. In particular, I accompanied the soloist, Geoffrey Lester, that Gospel singer with the most beautiful tenor voice.

Almost immediately, however, the same team of students as had been to Cowdenbeath were off to Troon in Ayrshire to Tom Fitch's church of St. Meddans for a mission there. By then I knew that I was tired, but had to continue, although something was working within me to cause me to compare all these missionary endeavours with what I was discovering as it were by accident. For I was realising that the steady ministry of the Word Sunday by Sunday was building souls up in their faith and developing qualities of Christian character which were increasingly obvious. The Word was clearly getting under people's skins. I was already beginning to see that it was such teaching of the Word and not what I have since called evangelisticism which was to be the God-given task of my life.

Not only so, but the euphoria which had characterised the community in the latter half of 1945 following the end of the War and into 1946 had begun to wane. There was a falling off of interest in the Saturday Rallies. Perhaps it was partly that we had well-nigh exhausted our resources in the way of evangelistic tricks to attract young people. Increasingly I knew that the preaching of the Word on the Lord's Day was taking a stronger grip on me, and I was much more conscious of the Lord's enabling as I preached the Word then than in running the Rallies on Saturday evenings. A conviction therefore grew within me that to foster this deeper preaching and teaching of the Word, we should rather spend our Saturday evenings in prayer.

It was not easy to intimate to the inter-denominational group involved in the Youth Rallies, including many students that we needed our halls for prayer on Saturday evenings, and it was therefore necessary for Youth for Christ to move out to other premises. It was also clear that I was to call a halt to my own involvement in the organisation. There was a great outcry among local evangelistic people about it and I was reviled for years over the matter - 'You are driving our young people into the cinema,' they protested (that was the last word in those days!), but I was sure that it was the Lord who guided, and I am glad to say the Youth for Christ continued in the local Y.M.C.A. for about ten successful years after that.

* * * * * *

But the change which took place at the beginning of 1947 with the start of Saturday prayer, along with the commencement of Daily Bible-reading Notes in the Congregational Record and the emphasis on systematic Bible preaching was so marked that there was no doubt that this was the way the Lord was leading.

It has to be admitted however that we lost almost immediately the support of perhaps two hundred or so attenders from other fellowships who had revelled in the evangelistic preaching, but were not so happy with the Word turned on the many Christians then around, namely themselves. To discover that there was love of evangelistic preaching which proved to be antagonistic to the deeper teaching of the Word was one of the most appalling shocks I have ever experienced. I still do not understand it, but there is no doubt about it. Yet it was gratifying that most of the students who had followed through, some from my own student days saw the significance of the move and remained faithful and true. It was from this early stage, therefore, that our congregation became and has remained ever since a students' church to generations of students, the bulk of the most faithful ones being associated with the University Christian Union, progressively changing its name from C.S.F., to Evangelical Union and Christian Union.

However, looking back, it ought to be said that the influence upon University students stemmed not only from Kings Chapel activities, but also from the fact that I had found time to represent the Divinity Students in the Students Representative Council (S.R.C.). In that capacity I had become involved in organising harvest employment for students during summer vacations (there being a shortage of labour on account of the War effort). This had occupied me throughout more than one summer. I had also become interested in the student publication, *Gaudie*, and from that I was appointed Director of Publications for the S.R.C. with periodic opportunities to write editorials for *Gaudie*.

Lastly, I had become widely known through my work on the students' annual theatre show which I orchestrated in my last year at Kings, 1944. Having related these exciting times I can only add that I have no personal record of this work having lost the musical score. It may still be lying in some remote cupboard of Marischal College!

All these activities may be said to have fitted me to work with students. Nonetheless, it is quite clear to me that where there is an appeal to the intellect as well as to the moral and spiritual conscience of thinking young people on the basis of the Word of God, there will always be some who will respond, and it is, I am convinced, the patient, persistent fostering of a love of the Word of God in the minds and hearts of young people which is the secret of leading them on both into God-given vocation and service for God.

There is a pulse in the Word of God created by its Author, the Holy Spirit, wherever you turn it up, which if the preacher begins to feel it, will quicken him and make his ministry of the Word not only living but attractive, even when it hurts, and which some will always cherish, however many turn away. Yet it also has to be said, that if a man 'pulls the punches' in his ministry of the Word because he desires mere popularity and with the motive purely of winning and attracting these intelligent young people who tentatively come along to consider his ministry, he will have no lasting effect on any. This man cannot bear to see them go when they are offended or bored. Yet those who eventually respond and become somebodies in the Lord's service are those who have been arrested and who may appear to react against all they hear; these are the ones who are often shocked by the force of the Word and things they never expected to hear, into creative and disturbing thought.

There is a magnetic repulsion/attraction about the Word which takes its own time to sort out people's thoughts. Do you not think that the rich young ruler eventually came back to Christ? I do! He who is not prepared to make enemies for Christ's sake by the faithful preaching of the Word will never make lasting friends for Christ, either.

For whatever reason, I have always felt very much at home with student young folk almost anywhere, and coming to Gilcomston having been out of Aberdeen only one year since my licensing, some of my later associates came at once to Gilcomston to worship with me. From that beginning my association with students at our church has grown and gone on ever since. In addition, our early fervour and unusual behaviour attracted attention elsewhere and soon requests to speak to student groups beyond Aberdeen came pouring in and I was always keen to oblige. Perhaps my interest in away engagements with students was because I sometimes felt that they were keener on what I was saying than many in those early days in the congregation at home - though not always. I certainly regarded my student engagements almost on a par with my ministry at Gilcomston and prepared very particularly for them.

When I look, however, at my diaries and see the number of home engagements, weddings, funerals, as well as a regular ministry to hungry congregations which filled my time during these years - even before and while student meetings became a spate - I marvel at how the Lord helped me to meet them all and yet remain fit for the ministry at Gilcomston. One reason for being able to run round the country so much and yet maintain the work at home is perhaps that I have learned to do one thing at a time and to do it with all my might, and then another, and another. Since I have ordered my life not to be taken up with trivia, all my time has been taken up with preparation for these meetings and services. It must be added that as our congregational life gradually became stripped to the bare essentials I was perhaps freer than other men to undertake this work. Without a plethora of other meetings to prepare for apart from the Sunday services, the mid-week Bible studies and the Saturday prayer meeting, I had time for these other things.

Yet I feel too that the students whom I met both at Gilcomston and beyond sensed that I was particularly interested in them. Was it that as a bachelor, not having settled down like a young married man with a growing family, I was able to give more time to them? I certainly think that whether it springs from a certain immaturity or not, I have always had a definite rapport with these young people and am often attributed with the gift of perpetual youth. From my vantage point of being in my eighty-first year it would certainly seem to be so! Yet, whatever the reason for its beginnings and its growth, I have always considered my student work, wherever it took me, as vital and when I think how many ministers and missionaries have come out of these years, it was all surely worth it.

Amongst the students I suppose that I have a particular interest in those young men who showed any signs of responding to the call to the ministry. Although I have learned to minister the Word to all and sundry and leave the results to the Lord since you never know all or even the most of what God is doing through your ministry, I have always felt that I had something to give those called in this way in particular: something I had found profitable in the task. It is interesting how the Lord chooses men at different stages in their lives, from childhood right on even to men of some maturity. Certainly my own chequered career up to twenty-nine years of age fitted me more to understand this variety amongst the students and to understand something of human nature once I was a minister. On one particular occasion when I was asked to give the Charge to Divinity students being licensed by Aberdeen Presbytery, I was able to talk on some of the things I have learned along the way. That Charge has been printed and reprinted several times since and reproduced in many periodicals. It contains a broad sweep of the work of the preacher of the Word and I believe has profited many.

* * * * * *

To go through these last forty six years and pick out the highlights of ministry to students is not easy, for there has been a consistency about their response which makes it hard to see peaks and troughs. There was the time when a large batch of young folk having come up from a certain kind of pietistic background with great emphasis on quiet-times and devotional exercises and with many shiboleths about what entertainments were allowed and what were not became so disillusioned and even bored with their Christian lives that one was forced to ask what was happening to them. They were getting tired of the kind of Christianity they had gathered from pietistic fellowships at home or at school or in church.

The truth was that their rigid pietism had turned them into little legalists, and for them the Christian life was a matter of strict quiet-times with sundry dos and don'ts, mostly don'ts. Nor could they understand what was wrong. Were they backsliding? No: they were getting tired of a rigid way of life which had lost the joy and verve and the whole dimension of grace. So a series of sermons was preached from Old Testament and New and later published as *The World of Grace*. These have seen many souls liberated from a life of petty rules into one of love and joy and hope of glory to come, as well as into costly, sacrificial and adventurous service for the Lord.

Perhaps it was from that time that the students of Aberdeen and progressively of other Universities began to see the relevance of the systematic teaching of the Word. As the diaries show, 1947 was almost as busy a year as 1946. It began with a New Year's Day Conference at Inverness Baptist Church, but by the 17th of the month I was speaking at Edinburgh University Christian Union and by the 14th of February at Glasgow University Christian Union.

That night I travelled by sleeper to London and on Saturday 15th spoke at Tom Rees's Youth Rally at Central Hall, Westminster, and then went on to stay the night at Hildenborough Hall, Tom's Youth Centre in Kent. The next day I was off to Leeds University to lead a Mission in the University there along with James Philip and Gill Struan

Marshall, at the opening of which the Principal of the University and Professor F. F. Bruce, still teaching there then, were present. I must say that I felt myself unfitted to undertake these responsibilities, having had so little schooling and not even one academic degree, and it could hardly be said that the Leeds Mission was a success. These were the specifically student meetings during the year, although I also spoke at the pre-Assembly Rally on the Lord's Day at St. Andrew's Church, Edinburgh in May; in June I was a speaker at the Portstewart Convention in Ulster; in September I undertook a week's teaching of Romans at Hildenborough Hall for Tom Rees and the same month spoke at the Glasgow Keswick-type Convention and in October, by then quite exhausted, at a Rally at Charlotte Chapel.

The next year, 1948 was a difficult year at home in Gilcomston because of the transition from evangelisticism to Bible teaching. The poor congregation must have wondered what they had let themselves in for with the radical changes both in preaching style and in congregation size which were occurring.

I had only one student meeting that year, although students were attending our services all the time; but that was at Oxford to the Inter-Collegiate Christian Union. I spoke at their Saturday Rally on February 7th and on Sunday evening preached in St. Mary the Virgin Church to a crowded student congregation and thereafter dealt with a highly cultured young gentleman who was obviously seeking. I hoped he came through to vital faith.

Interestingly enough the only student meeting out of Aberdeen in 1949, which was also a difficult year at home, was at Cambridge in the month of May to the Inter-Collegiate Christian Union there. That invitation came through the C.I.C.C.U.'s President, George May who had been converted as a student in our Church Hall in 1946. He was brought to us the first time by a keen soul-seeking fellow and he opened his heart spontaneously to the Lord. I have often instanced George with others as an example of how readily the Word of God converts souls in any situation in which it is released by the Holy Spirit through prayer. The idea that the 'bones' of the Gospel must be presented before anyone can be converted is nonsense. The Lord is constantly seeking his own, and finds them by his Word released through the prayer of faith. I was asked to speak then on 1 Peter 3, a difficult chapter, but did not deal adequately with the different interpretations, alas. When I think now of how I foisted my bare knowledge on people simply because I was keen, I am shocked. Yet the Lord used some of it.

Thus my association with students and my involvement in a specific student ministry grew. Throughout the 1940s and 50s there was a steady increase with the busiest times coming in the 60s and 70s. By the 1980s I was beginning to feel that all the junketing about the country was rather too exerting for one of my years - although I have continued with some engagements!

One of the events during these years to have a great impact upon the evangelical community in Scotland and in particular amongst the young was Billy Graham's Kelvin Hall Crusade in 1955. I attended an evening meeting of this campaign when the Duke and Duchess of Hamilton were on the platform. I conducted relay meetings from that Crusade in Aberdeen in Gilcomston for a week and also at Fort William, as well as organising counselling for the Pittodrie Rally on that freezing cold night in May!

James Philip had been instrumental in getting the Assembly to invite Billy Graham to Scotland and the local organisation of the one night stand at Pittodrie in Aberdeen was in the hands of the Presbytery. Although I was active by then in the Central Churches Association along with men like David Doeg of Holburn Central, there was still such suspicion of what I would do on such an evangelistic occasion that I was excluded from participation in the central organisation! Although our emphasis by that time was on the systematic exposition of the Word, the Presbytery could not easily forget my early flight into frenzied Gospel preaching. Eventually, however, they relented and actually gave me the counselling at the football stadium to do.

On the night, when it was so freezing cold, after Billy preached, I had to see to it that all the counsellors were on the alert as people began to trickle and then to stream forward. I suppose I ran right round that football ground half a dozen times during the latter part of the evening making sure that everyone who had come forward had a counsellor.

Before the 1955 meeting, however, I had sent Billy a note in some concern about some of his associations with people in this country who were far from conservative. Although he never mentioned it, indeed I don't even know if he even received the note, I felt that it affected his greeting of me then. No doubt he thought that I had become exceedingly narrow in the intervening years since his last visit. (I am glad to say, however, that on his return in May, 1991 he was kind enough to call with Cliff Barrows and we spent the best part of two hours reminiscing and in discussion. In particular we talked at some length about the coming of the Lord in relation to Romans 11:12,15,25,26.)

The work amongst students continued to grow during these years and I was often away from home for a large part of any one week. An example of this activity was in April and May 1959 when I spoke to Edinburgh E.U. on the *Moral and Social Implications of the Gospel* in the afternoon, and to the Graduates' Fellowship later on *Paul, a Changed Man*. Next day, the 24th, the subject at Aberdeen Evangelical Union was *Demonology*, and on 4th May I was back in Edinburgh speaking to Moray House College of Education on the subject of *Temptation*. On the 15th I was away again to Inverness, speaking to the Y.M.C.A. on *The Inspiration of the Word of God*. On the following day I was at St. Andrews E.U. on Hebrews 13.8,9 on the *Grace of Jesus Christ* - the same, yesterday, today and for ever.

It was a reflection, I think, of the keenness and hunger of the Christian Unions that they provided their speakers with so many challenging and satisfying subjects to speak on. On very few occasions did they fail to suggest a topic or passage on which to speak and seldom did I have to query what they had requested. The subjects were generally those that one could deal with in some depth and saw would be useful to the students. I think that it is remarkable that having some idea of what students needed, I had so seldom to tell them what they required. They seemed to know, although sometimes they didn't and needed to be told.

Some meetings, of course, were more memorable than others and I recall one occasion at the Graduates' Fellowship Conference at Bush House in Edinburgh where the theme was to be *Methods of Evangelism*. My contribution wasn't all that acceptable because by then our method of evangelism was what I call primary: that of being built up in the faith and living the life where one is and letting that tell, not least because some of the finest servants of the Lord who had come forth by then were won that way. Perhaps the person who issued the invitations was unaware of the thrust of my ministry by that time. They were certainly aware of it by the time the conference was over!

A meeting which was memorable for entirely different

reasons was in 1967 when I spoke to the students of Aberdeen Union at Ballater in November. Some weeks earlier the Lord had taken my aged Mother home and as I spoke on the final days of Christ from John, chapters 11-13 I recall how tender-hearted I felt and close to tears. Although she had been unwell for years and had suffered a massive heart attack some fourteen years previously, she had sat under my ministry for many years. I had often teased her about being my keenest Bible student as she consulted great books and commentaries, and in church listened with avid attention. She, with Auntie, had been my most ardent supporters, particularly through the difficult early years. Neither were ever to know how much I really valued their loving, unconditional support.

In 1973 I made my first visit to John Kelly's Bangor group of young people. This took place during the first days of July, and I had the privilege of addressing three times a day for five days as keen a group of young people, mostly students, as ever I have met. This I did during either July or August for six successive years, and it has been one of the inspirations of my life and ministry. These return visits to places of initial blessing have often been particularly encouraging, witnessing growth and change taking place in the lives of these young people, something in the round of engagements which I was not always privileged to see.

A topic which was often discussed at various meetings across the country was the political situation and its relation to the Word of God. On several occasions issues such as the Communist threat, the Middle East and nuclear disarmament amongst nations crept into talks on other matters or came into the conversation after a meeting. Throughout the years I have certainly felt a great deal about the Soviet menace in particular and in 1961 I was compelled to speak on it at the London Bible College and at the Bible Training Institute, Glasgow a day or

two later. At that time the USSR was waving the banner and
frightening everyone with the bomb. Kruschev was banging
his shoe on the table of the United Nations and before long the
whole Cuba situation had arisen. It seemed to me that at the
rate of the progress of the USSR's power and influence we
would soon be overrun. Did we need to prepare a church for
persecution? I swithered then between two things - indeed
three possibilities: the Lord could come and take us all away
before the end of the century; there could be revival (and
holding the view I do about the Lord's return, I look for
revival); or, there could be a new dark age, a thousand years
of darkness. It was a frightening time.

Throughout the years we have prayed a great deal for
Christians behind the Iron Curtain and it is therefore a great
thing that the threat has been rolling away in recent years.
Nevertheless, I have no doubt that Israel is the key to
international politics and in particular in the Middle East. I
have little doubt about the coming conversion of Israel to
Christ and believe that God has brought them back to their
homeland with a view to their conversion. Thus all the Arabs
and Palestinians can do will not shift Israel, since her dogged-
ness, at its best, is surely from God.

My health suffered in subsequent years when I suffered a
heart attack having rushed home to Aberdeen at 1.30 in the
morning after a sequence of four meetings in different cities
in as many days. I awoke in the middle of the night with a
terrific pain and I knew that it was my heart. It got worse till
I was so ill I couldn't lift the telephone to summon help. I just
lay there and waited for expiry. Finally, however, it subsided
and I fell asleep. Somewhat weak next morning I visited my
doctor where it was confirmed that I had had a moderately
severe heart attack and there was some damage. I was hastily
ordered to take it easy and shed my load as far as possible: I

had to lose weight and cut down on my work. For years thereafter I could be found most mornings walking round the suburbs of the city at about 6 a.m. I also took the chance to speak to Aberdeen students during this time rather than travel. It has never seriously bothered me since although I have had one or two stabs of pain occasionally and still get periodic cardiographs to monitor proceedings.

A friend of mine, David Short who was Consultant Physician in Aberdeen for years warned me sternly about my health during this period. I met David Short at a function not so long ago and asked him whether he expected me still to be alive! I think that he was a little taken aback and did not give me an answer but I am sure that he did not expect to see me survive for many years, far less the nineteen years I have been not only alive but more active than ever.

* * * * * *

There had to come a time, therefore, when I was unable to continue with as many away engagements and had to consider winding down my student commitment beyond Gilcomston. I think it was largely age which made me feel, not that I was growing old and less interested - I am keener than ever now at eighty and my mind feels sharper than ever - but travelling about was more of a burden.

My life was also narrowing more to Gilcomston and my ministry there. Also, others were doing these things so I was not needed so much any more. There was also this charismatic thing growing and many students thought our ministry too hard for them. I began to fear for the Christian Unions and still am concerned about them, although the closeness of the Aberdeen committees to Gilcomston has mostly meant that I could discuss their plans for speakers with them and advise. The rise of solid young folk in Dundee C.U. in recent years (after a gap) has also shown that there is still a hunger for something solid. Of course, there are now sufficient ministries in the Church of Scotland nationwide to ensure that even if the C.U. went 'off', the work would continue, and biblical ministries would still produce men and women of character and prepare them for service. I feel sorry for able men in the ministry who find themselves in situations in which they lose such young folk to University and College cities, such as Aberdeen. If the work has done something, however, for the Church of Scotland then it has been to supply men for the ministry largely from the student fraternity which I have encountered either sitting in church, or earlier, on student engagements.

The plan to call a halt to this work began really in 1986 which involved only one student meeting, to the local T.S.F. I intended it to be my final swansong as far as student meetings were concerned. In 1989, however, I was still doing the odd meeting and gave an address to the local C.U. on Genesis 3 but it was simply because several of the Committee who were dear to me prevailed on me to do so. Surely my last swansong!

As I have said, there has always been a student community in Gilcomston during term-time with a large number of Divinity students amongst them. As I have attended fewer and fewer away meetings, it has been a joy for me to have so many young folk round me here at home.

Some would say that the early attendance of old University friends does not explain the steady attendance of students during forty six years of ministry there, but that the ministry was such as appealed to keen young people. Whether that is so or not, we have never been without our constituency of students more or less, and it is of these largely, along with nurses and others, that the outreaches beyond Aberdeen and overseas to the Lord's service have taken place.

Indeed, long before the Inter Varsity Fellowship (now the University and Colleges Christian Fellowship) began to be concerned over the appalling wastage of students going down from University and College and failing to integrate into local church life there was a pattern of life at Gilcomston which often vied with the Christian Union for their chief interest. In fact there were times when I felt it my duty to advise young students that their prior responsibility as students was to attend to the evangelisation of their University or College: they could devote themselves to church life thereafter. That had always been my intention as a student myself. Nonetheless, since a Christian Union over so many years sees many fortunes good and ill, I was not sorry that the cream of these young folk were intent upon the Bible teaching ministry to build themselves up in their holy faith. It is certainly of these that the most fruitful servants of the Lord I have known have been found.

Of course, since the aim of the ministry from nearly its inception was to form a people, at first largely nominal, into a Christian congregation, and as soon as possible into a fellowship of like-minded believers to love the Lord and his Word, and then even more integrally into a larger Christian family - since that is what I conceive a true church to be - it was easier for students, most of them away from home to integrate with a people ever seeking to grow warmer in fellowship and more co-operative and hospitable.

Undoubtedly there have been times when the number of students tended to dominate the fellowship, especially the younger folk, and since students had their own corporate life at University and College and knew one another well, they tended sometimes to become cliquish, and doubtless were unaware that they made non-Varsity young folk feel somewhat inferior.

That had to be dealt with as tactfully as possible, although it was not until we ripped out our pews and refloored and carpeted the church building and installed moveable chairs that the different intellectual categories and age groups began somehow really to integrate. It is exciting to see how simple changes in architecture and dynamics can effect the fellowship of believers: now young mix with old and old with young in most wonderful fellowship, in which the care of some of these young folk for aged attenders in their seventies, eighties and even nineties is most wonderful to see! I can think of a ninety-two year old who has so many of the young folk buzzing around her after the evening service that the young people, finding her so interesting and full of kindly humour and interest in their welfare have almost to queue up to speak with her.

I suppose the way to make people feel at home is for the minister, believing that the Lord has set him in that very place to build a Church (and I certainly was absolutely sure of that!), himself to feel at home, and make those around him feel at home also and welcome. This can be done in many ways, but I am sure that the fact that the minister was sure of his call to that congregation helped those who were there and who came in to begin to feel something of the settledness of the fellowship, and that that enabled a work to proceed without distraction. Nothing is so damaging to a company of the Lord's people as to feel that their future is uncertain and its leadership insecure. The psychological and spiritual effect of being settled and assured, I believe, cannot be over-estimated. I believe that through the many years this has been one of the most stabilising factors in our whole situation.

Then again, a great emphasis in a truly balanced biblical ministry is bound to be the sacredness of the domestic family. And as families have formed and in time their young people are integrated into the life of the Church as their spiritual home, the quality of home life has improved, and the challenge in the Word constantly to keep open and hospitable house and to receive strangers in the hope that one may be entertaining angels unawares has led to a number of our families, though not all, preparing at the week-ends particularly, to entertain visitors at church to meals at their homes. Many have deliberately prepared food beforehand for such emergencies, and therefore on a Sunday morning especially, potential hosts and hostesses will be looking around as the congregation assembles and afterwards to see who they may invite to lunch and possibly entertain for the rest of the day and bring to Church again in the evening if they so desire.

I have known students and others, notably of the oil industry, who years afterwards have recalled that the very first Sunday they attended our congregation they were invited to lunch, which gracious action alone inclined them to think and feel that that would be a good place to worship.

One of the thrills on a Sunday evening is to see how soon new people, who appear by their regularity to have committed themselves to the fellowship are enlisted to help with such menial tasks as the serving of tea from the side tables in the actual church building. Such service by young men as well as young women soon makes the people taking part feel at home, and helps the process of the Word of God reaching from minds to hearts and then to hands and feet and lips.

Two of the things which have impressed me through the years as most remarkable and unexpected especially for an old bachelor (and these are of wider interest than that of students and probably belong strictly-speaking to another part of this volume) is firstly, to find young children brought up in godly homes so advanced in their understanding of the faith and the holy Scriptures; and secondly, how easy it is in gracious

circumstances where the Word is in the ascendant for all ages
to mix well with absolutely nothing of that segregation of
groups or categories which most people seem to think important and inevitable in congregational life.

It is not so: whole denominations and their congregations
have been ruined by adopting habits which become unthink-
ing traditions of breaking up the natural fellowship between
different age groups, sexes and interests which obtains in
family life. As our church structure has become devoid of
these groupings - we have no meetings other than Sunday
services with a Sunday school for the under-eights, a mid-
week Bible study and a Saturday night prayer meeting - we
have found more family-like fellowship than ever before.
Where this unity does not exist but various groups are formed
something approaching a clan system operates, until all that
these congregations have is a series of isolated coteries, call
them guilds or clubs or fellowships or whatever, often with
one-track minds concentrating on their own inturned huddles
so that individuals of one group would hardly dare to look at
individuals of another group with the eyes of mercy; and if one
group pinched another's night of the church hall or used its
equipment, there were ructions! What a lot of unpsychological
and irrational nonsense! Divide and perish! No! Instead,
Unite and live!

One thing which I have always attempted to do is to
maintain the same preaching methods and style whether
students are present or not. It was never the case that I
preached differently over the summer or throughout other
non-term times of the year. Sometimes I have wondered as we
approached October whether another dose of Romans would
be good for them, or I have wondered what I would do in July,
August and September when they were away, but not to any
significant extent. This is the thing about the systematic

expository preaching of the Word that it goes sweetly on through thick and thin and it is in the course of ranging widely through the Scriptures that one comes upon exciting things, whatever the time of year.

Beyond all this, there is the service of counselling young folk mainly as a result of what the Word of God throws up in a Bible teaching ministry. That has to be discussed privately. After services, especially the evening service when there is more time, hours may be spent counselling. And yet, it is astonishing to find, that as the Word takes hold of individuals, one sees young folk who formerly were full of difficulties and problems coming to me less and less, because they are learning from their study and acceptance of the saving and sanctifying Word to apply the Word to their own problems.

Nonetheless such areas as biblical understanding and application are often discussed after particular services as well as more personal issues such as vocations and relationships. In the matter of friendships and incipient courtships as well as problems encountered with unconverted parents at home much love and time is required with often more listening than advising taking place. Similarly, deeper emotional or moral problems are discussed although many prefer the privacy of Beaconsfield Place for the more painful of these issues. Denominational problems such as baptism, the Lord's Supper and membership are also discussed, all of which call for time and much thought and prayer.

Sometimes problems are so deep and intractably difficult that others with specialised knowledge have to be called in, such as medical doctors, psychiatrists, lawyers, professional theologians and the like, and as I have said, arrangements are made for appointments at other times in the manse, where in the quietness of one-to-one sharing, issues often of a distressing nature can be discussed at leisure.

During the first five years of the ministry I also had the help
of Auntie in this task of counselling. Indeed, she became a
'mother in Israel' to the many young people who crowded our
church in those days. It was not unusual for the door bell to
ring and on answering to be told, 'It's not you I want to see,
Mr. Still, but Mrs. Alexander.' Many a serious and fruitful
conversation was conducted at the kitchen fireside during
those happy and exciting years, as many now out in the Lord's
service today would acknowledge. Auntie was 'greatly beloved', and those two words are engraved on her tombstone.

One thing is vastly important, and that is that by one's air
of deep interest in those attending church one seeks to convey
to people one's readiness to help - and yet without the slightest
suggestion of breathing down their necks, or of interfering in
private lives, or of rejoicing in a clientele or in enjoying the
establishment of a following.

With regard to the friendships of young people, especially
between the sexes, it is important while seeing what may be
going on, say, after services, to take absolutely no overt notice
of these things until obliged to do so by some approach.

Anything in the nature of snooping on youngsters would
be immediately frowned upon by them, and would surely
drive them away. And even when one is consulted, a certain
restraint is necessary, lest young folk gain the impression that
one is anxious to enlist their adherence and to fashion them
into some common mould which could be the pet interest of
the pastor.

Any suggestion that young folk might be fodder for
membership should be studiously avoided. I find it necessary
in showing genuine interest in young people, even if they
appear from other fellowships, to go to extremes not to show
the slightest interest in grabbing them, but simply accept their
probable occasional appearance as welcome visitors without

the slightest interest in sheep stealing. To be adviser to those committed to other fellowships and to encourage members or adherents to be faithful to their ministers and congregations is surely pleasing to God, and never - no, never to criticise other ministries, even when invited to do so. Sheep stealers often at length suffer from other sheep stealers!

One problem which I have mentioned which is often raised by young folk converted through Scripture Union, Crusaders, or other evangelical agencies during childhood or early youth is relations with unconverted or uncommitted parents. This has to be handled with great care, asking more questions than pronouncing opinions.

I often say to people consulting me, 'I never give advice:' the most I can do is having listened sympathetically, to advise believers to find their counsel where I find mine, from God by his Holy Word and by his Holy Spirit. The aim is to help people see what the Lord is saying to them - not to tell them what you think, which could turn out to be utterly inappropriate. At least this assures people seeking help that their personalities and individuality are being respected, and that one has no interest in giving stock answers to peculiarly personal problems. Indeed it is important to receive every fresh approach as something one has never met before, and therefore shed all preconceived notions and prejudices as to what the solution and answer may be in particular cases.

To have the privilege of being the confidant of precious young souls brought to Christ or coming to Christ is a heavy responsibility, and only God himself can enable the faithful discharge of such an onerous responsibility. God help us!

CHAPTER 11

THE EXPOSITORY MINISTRY

My experience of any controversy or even differing opinions over biblical scholarship was virtually nil until I began to train for the Church of Scotland ministry in 1939. Up until that point my upbringing and training had been in the Salvation Army where exclusive concentration was on what we might call 'initial evangelism', leaving much of the Word of God undiscovered and untaught. Even in the Salvation Army Training College in London which I attended for just over a term until my health broke down, the teaching as I recall it was sketchy. Too often in such evangelical circles the Gospel was reduced to a set of familiar texts which if one did not use, one was 'not preaching the Gospel', a remark still made today in unenlightened circles. My knowledge, therefore, was centred on these well-known texts, the evangelistic cliches and Sankey-type songs.

The inspiration behind this evangelistic Gospel may well have come from men like Spurgeon, Moody and William Booth, and its worthy aim was to win the lost for Jesus Christ. During the late nineteenth and early twentieth centuries the Kirk was preoccupied with what she believed about the Bible (dilemmas largely exported from the German church) and was subsequently distracted from her primary tasks of preaching the Gospel and teaching the Word of God. One can readily understand why a great deal of Christian zeal and endeavour began to be concentrated outside the Kirk at that time in para-church bodies like the Y.M.C.A. and Mission Halls of one kind or another.

Yet use of the Bible as a whole and teaching its truth was largely unknown, certainly to me. Although there was 'holiness teaching' in the Salvation Army it was of an Arminian order, with an undue preoccupation with the inward spiritual condition. It laid down rigid rules of behaviour which, alas, often strayed from true sanctification to petty legalism - even double standards: one for the public testimony meeting, and another for private and personal life. It was not until I came to University and associated with the local Union of the Inter Varsity Fellowship, the C.S.F., and with young people of other denominations that I began to see what a wealth there was in the Word of God for a far more enriching understanding of the Christian life and the Christian Church than I had known before.

In addition, I became aware of the deep divisions between liberal and conservative Protestant factions even within the University. Through my involvement in both groups I learned that the C.S.F. looked askance at the S.C.M. for its liberal standpoint and the S.C.M. considered the C.S.F., in contrast, to be narrow minded and 'behind the times'. I discovered that although the S.C.M. had at first been evangelical, it had begun to open its doors so widely to 'seekers' after the Truth that it was often a critical and sociological debating group rather than one taking an assured biblical and evangelical stance.

Yet, just as my eyes were being opened under the influence of Inter Varsity associates, not only at Aberdeen but with students and staff of other Universities whom I met at Conferences, I was plunged after two years of Arts into the Divinity Hall of Christ's College Aberdeen. There I was made aware of the other side of biblical scholarship. During my

three years there my increasing understanding about the
Christian life and the Word of God was repeatedly chal-
lenged, faced as I was with a certain amount of liberal
teaching. It must be said that for all the knowledge I was
acquiring it did not add up in any significant way to a
deepening understanding of the Word of God. Rather it led to
confusion and a dissipation of my zeal and early convictions.
These years indeed were a time of inner intellectual and
spiritual conflict between my evangelical beliefs and what I
read and heard from lecturers and more liberal friends.
Perhaps mirroring this tension these were also years of ardent
Christian activity and an increasing number of musical exploits.

It is hardly surprising perhaps that I left Aberdeen for my
assistantship at Springburnhill Parish Church, Glasgow in a
somewhat cynical frame of mind. As I have related, the
subsequent months first found me struggling against the
strong minded and forceful evangelicalism of my 'bishop',
William Fitch, and then returning with enthusiasm after my
crippling accident to my desire to serve Christ wherever he
placed me.

How my mind crystalised in such a manner during those
months of inactivity remains a mystery to me but there was no
question about the burning zeal in my breast as I began in
Gilcomston South in 1945. I would be a flaming evangelist!
The treasurer who had sought to engineer my coming to
Gilcomston said, 'He will fill the Kirk,' but he could hardly
have anticipated my methods. My declaration at my Induction
that I would want to inscribe the words, 'Christ Crucified'
over the Gothic arch of that beautiful sanctuary was me
nailing my colours to the mast before the gathering of local
ministers who were present.

And so I began. Since the place was so run down that it was

twice threatened with closure, the handful of keen officebearers pleaded with me to do anything I could to raise a crowd - such as I had done with musical recitals in various churches during the war years in Aberdeen in my student days.

I doubt if a rather fierce attack on the town of an evangelistic nature was what they expected or wanted; but that is what they got. And I did fill the Kirk - to overflowing, by the use of Redemption songs and fiery evangelistic sermons which soon set the town agog! All my old evangelistic zeal arose and away I went preaching the Gospel as I had been brought up with it, often in the most lurid Salvation Army fashion - the texts of sermons, and those inscribed on the huge notice board outside the Church bear witness to the fiery impact made, not only upon the congregation which then began to swell, but on Union Street and upon the Presbytery, many of whom began to frown upon this rather brash evangelistic approach. That went on for eighteen months which included visits to the town and to Gilcomston of various evangelists including Billy Graham and Alan Redpath.

I am glad of all that now for in the aftermath of the second world war, which ended in the year of my Induction in 1945, I tried the evangelistic method as few had done in church situations. Yet by a means utterly beyond my ken, but rationally due to the difference between even superficial exposition of the Scriptures at Sunday services and Gospel attempts at united Saturday rallies, I gradually came to the conclusion towards the end of 1946 that there was something vastly superior about the systematic exposition of the Scriptures to the evangelistic ministry.

For 1946 had been a feverishly active year. In March Billy Graham and his team had descended upon us with the consequent organisation of the Youth for Christ rallies. I began addressing some gatherings beyond Aberdeen, not least the Keswick type meetings held in Edinburgh in July. This had drained me considerably and was followed immediately by the red-hot campaign in Cowdenbeath. Alan Redpath's Mission was in October and then I was away again to Troon with Tom Fitch the following month. Then it was back to Gilcomston to plan for the Christmas services and to attempt to arrange a Watch Night programme which would satisfy the attenders and outstrip the previous year's success.

Perhaps it was the Alan Redpath Mission in the Music Hall which did most to disillusion me with these big campaigns and contrast them with what I was finding to be the fruits of solid congregational work. It was the biggest evangelistic project in Aberdeen since the Lionel Fletcher Campaign. Although many were converted, tensions arose from it which could only be distressing and which did not help the work. Much of it seemed to arise from the differing styles of the two leaders. Alan Redpath was a former rugby player who preached as he played while Geoffrey Lester who sang during the meetings in his rich tenor voice was a complete contrast. We did not know until afterwards that there were tensions between these two although they did continue to work together thereafter. More locally, a split developed in the Aberdeen Evangelistic Association with one denomination unable to agree to the basis on which the group met and another unhappy about such exclusiveness. All this did nothing to ease relations amongst the churches in the city.

Although the congregation was collectively involved in the campaign, my main responsibility was to accompany Geoffrey on the piano during the meetings and on the organ at his lunch time recitals in West St. Andrew's Church. This continued for three weeks during which time our own Sunday evening service was changed from its usual hour to suit the campaign meetings and was poorly attended as a result. Only a handful attended these brief services at six o'clock and as the three weeks drew to a close I knew that I was getting fed up with it and was weary to return to our own work. By the final Sunday evening I was tired and was also aware that they were preparing for a build up for the last night which suggested to me a parade of trophies and I hadn't the heart for it. In fact, I felt that I could not go for after our own service something said to me clearly, 'You are not going to the Music Hall tonight for the final round up' and I was happy to comply. I was not particularly needed that evening anyway and so after our service I went to see my mother who had not been very well. Judge of my astonishment the next day when I heard that there had been a hue and cry for the minister of Gilcomston to open his church to cope with the overflow of those who had turned up at the Music Hall. But where was the minister?

The next day Alan Redpath called on me and demanded an explanation. I do not know if I said very much or if I explained my feelings and I certainly did not confide in him all my growing reservations about campaign meetings. More and more I was being dissatisfied with much of what passed for evangelistic work. I am sure that he found me unsatisfactory and although we worked together again at a mission in Springburn organised largely by William Fitch, he was never so cordial and I understood why.

It took a great struggle to come to the point where I knew that I had to call a halt to the Saturday night Rallies in the church. Yet it was with profound relief that I did so for they had been preying on my mind for some time. It was obvious that the necessity for maintaining a high level of novelty was too time-consuming and was taking up too much of our energies. I was tired of trying to be an evangelistic entertainer and compared it unfavourably with the more serious work on Sunday's when a sense of the Lord's presence came upon me

in power. There, souls were turning to Christ. They were
being drawn by the Word. After the service I would speak for
hours with some in the vestry. I remember walking up the
street late one Sunday night as if I was treading on air so great
was the wonder and excitement of pointing seekers to Christ.
I knew that I looked forward to the Sundays yet was growing
to dread the Saturday nights. It was if I was being told, 'This,
and not that!' It was not, as I see it now, that I was condemning
the one in favour of the other, but that the Lord was saying to
me, 'This is the way for you. Whatever other people do, you
do this, not that!'

It also seemed that the Rallies had lost some of their grip
on outsiders and had become more of a means of keeping
Christian young folk occupied on a Saturday night. The more
worldly manifestations had worried me from the beginning
but now it seemed that they had ceased to justify their
evangelistic existence and it could be not be right to continue
hosting such an obsolete event in Gilcomston.

I have already noted how, at the beginning of 1947 I
approached the Youth for Christ people one Saturday night
and announced that we needed our premises on Saturday
nights to devote ourselves to prayer. This was the beginning
of the change in the ministry and it coincided with the start of
our own Daily Bible Reading Notes. Roy Miller who worked
with Scripture Union in Aberdeen at that time gave me the
idea and impetus to begin. He had suggested various systems
of Daily Bible Readings including Scripture Union's and
several others, but concluded by asking, 'Why not write your
own?' I looked aghast at him. 'My own?'

Coaxed by him, however, to consider it, I dared to begin
the shortest notes ever written on John's Gospel, merely one
line a day in many cases, and thus the Daily Reading Notes
began - and have continued to this day!

Simultaneously, however, with the beginning of the prayer meeting and the opposition this new venture received, and as the Daily Bible Reading Notes started, a more fundamental change was now discernable. For some months I had been aware that something else was happening in Gilcomston or perhaps needed to happen. Increasingly I was becoming weary of the simple Gospel, not least because I had so many converts on my hands and they needed to be fed. Who was going to feed them? 'You,' said the Lord. It was as simple as that.

If I said eighteen months' experience of ardent evangelistic work caused disillusionment, that was only part of the truth, and was really beside the point. The truth is, as I have said, that I was beginning to discover, almost by accident although I know the Lord has another name for it, the value of the systematic teaching of the Word of God. And as that took grip of me in the pulpit during the latter days and months of 1946, I saw that a commission was given me, which was to be my task for the rest of my life, rather than that of superficial evangelism which, alas, leaves so much of the glorious Word of God untouched. And if it is true, which I fervently believe (and with some experience to back up my opinion) that there is no part of the Word of God which can be left out if fully rounded Christian characters are to be formed, then there is no alternative to ministering the whole Word of God.

The difference between 'using' the Bible for evangelistic material and setting out systematically to expound it in its entirety is so great that if I had seen the change from the one to the other in those radical terms when I started, I think I would have been daunted. Fortunately the Lord is wiser than to load upon us from the beginning all he purposes for us. It was exceedingly tentatively that I began what has turned out to be my life's work.

Of course, in combination with the ending of my involvement in Youth for Christ, this new ministry lost me almost at a stroke a following of nearly two hundred ardent evangelicals who had gathered round the Evangel as traditionally declared. But when I suddenly turned the Word of God on them, in its fullness and not in the form of carefully selected Gospel texts ('Gospel shots' the Salvation Army used to call them), most of them fled - though, as I have said, not the students.

Therefore one of the most humiliating experiences of my life had to be endured in those early months of 1947. Indeed within a couple of Sundays I lost a popular following and had to content myself with a far smaller constituency of attenders, since the numbers which at first crowded our church building largely disappeared. It was as sudden as that. The cry went up, 'He's finished already!' Actually, as I see it now, I was just beginning what has turned out to be, albeit costly, the most blessed portion of my life.

* * * * * *

The astonishing thing to my mind is that the systematic exposition of the Scriptures, now the norm in many ministries in Scotland and beyond, began for me in the most fortuitous fashion. I did not know then that Martyn Lloyd-Jones had adopted it at Westminster Chapel (although being in London at the time, I had attended the actual service at which he took over from Dr. Campbell Morgan), but I literally stumbled on it, surely by divine providence.

Undoubtedly there are endless texts for evangelistic sermons in the Bible, but it was in searching for the means to determine a sequence of sermons rather than spend so much time exercising the mind and scouring the Scriptures for suitable gospel themes that I must have chosen a book. Thus Galatians was first introduced on the morning of 5th January.

It was simply the finding of a text one week, and next week thinking I would follow it up with the next verse or passage that the thought of sequence excited me, and also, I noticed, interested some in the congregation. Remark was made that I had followed on from one passage to the next, and that, they said, was interesting!

By March I had completed Galatians and begun on James and then chapters in Romans were essayed. By the time 1948 had begun the pattern was pretty well established and Hebrews was the next book to be tackled.

I should add that these sequences of sermons only occurred in the Sunday morning services and this continued as far as the summer of 1950. We continued up until that point on the principal that one fed believers in the morning and evangelised sinners in the evening. One recalls the story of two ministers of St. George's Edinburgh - Alexander Whyte who 'blackened the saints in the morning' and James Black who 'whitened the sinners in the evening'! Gradually, however, in both morning and evening we pursued various books in this serial fashion as it was clear that this was a good way to study the Bible and in time to gain a balanced view of the whole Scriptural field. It has gone on ever since with occasional excursions into thematic or topical series. Sometimes for a complete change themes such as Parables, Miracles, Old Testament Characters, The Holy Spirit, What it means to be a Christian, The World of Grace, and such like have been followed and these were generally introduced to meet some immediate congregational need. Yet always there has been a return to the selection of a book and to the attempt to thoroughly master its contents, sequentially, week by week.

Yet how did the congregation react to this upturn? Think what it must have meant to unsuspecting nominal members of Gilcomston, first to be yanked utterly bewildered into the evangelistic set-up and then within two years to be ushered into the beginnings of the Bible teaching ministry. However hungry the new converts in the congregation were for the solid food of teaching, there were many others who were far from keen and who would put any obstacle in our way. Thus the years following this abrupt turn around in the ministry were never easy. Even until 1960 these struggles went on from time to time and have been stirred up intermittently ever since when the Word, in at least a little depth and ranging through the whole biblical revelation, has been ministered.

It was perhaps most difficult to deal with disagreements within the Kirk Session where ill feeling could often be felt more strongly than anywhere else. On these occasions it was necessary to root out the evil and I recall one incident when I felt almost sick with fear as to what they would do. It arose out of a very innocuous secular Choral Society which had been set up by a prominent man in the town who had actually helped Gilcomston to get off the ground and who had subsequently joined us and become an elder. His interest in music had led to this venture and many of the chief officebearers and members in the church had joined it. The practices, however were to be held on a Monday evening which was the night of our monthly officebearers meeting. A senior officebearer got up at one meeting and plausibly suggested that the church meeting be changed from Monday to Thursday. I asked, 'Why ought our meeting to be changed? Tell us why. Why can't you come?'

Although the conductor and his wife (we had women deacons then) were sitting there in the court, nobody would say. I pressed someone in the company to explain and to give a good reason but no one would, even although a number of the choir were also there. This went on for about half and hour. No one would come clean. Finally, I knew that I had to challenge them openly and I said, 'Well, if you, the officebearers of this church want a statutory meeting of our court to be changed from a Monday to a Thursday because you have a prior engagement with what is a secular society, and you put that before a meeting of the Lord's church, then I can no longer be your minister.' Inside, for all my brave face, I was thinking, 'This is the end. I'm for it!' and I knew that my knees were knocking and there was no pulpit to hide them. It was the most critical moment of my ministry for I knew that I was not merely challenging their support for the Session but their support for the ministry, myself, and all that we stood for.

Imagine my relief when they dropped it like a hot potato and it was never mentioned again. Some members of the court persisted in going to their Monday evening practices but that soon became odious in the fellowship and it stopped. I felt it was necessary, however, to write on the following morning to that choral conductor to tell him in no uncertain language what I thought of him, allowing one of his choir to make this move while he sat there without a word. By next post I received a request for his transference certificates. It was a very sad affair for I dearly loved that man and his family having known them for years. It was one of the sorest blows of my life because not only the church but soon the whole town knew about it. Yet I knew that it was *the* test of my mettle, and God vindicated that action, and years afterwards he and I were reconciled.

On other occasions the opposition was more overt such as when a number of the elders were speaking against the Gospel and in particular against the Saturday night prayer meeting. Naturally these men did not attend. So difficult did it become that I determined to speak out from the pulpit and one Friday night I was so burdened about it that I prepared a written manuscript, perhaps for the first time ever, to read out on the

Sunday. The following day was the Sunday School picnic and as I looked round at the men in question who were there I thought, 'If you knew what was coming to you tomorrow, you wouldn't come!' I remember I slipping away from the picnic to read and pray over that sermon with a heavy heart.

When the next day came I read this paper at the end of the service. 'There you sit,' I said, 'with your heads down, guilty men. What would you say if I named you before the whole congregation? You stand condemned before God for your contempt of his Word and of his folk.' The moment I had finished I walked out of the pulpit. There was no last hymn - no benediction. I went right home. It was the hardest and most shocking thing I have ever had to do in Gilcomston.

That week seven elders resigned and the Presbytery wanted to know all about it. What was going on? Twice I was called before Presbytery committees although it went no further. I think they just shook their heads and said, 'It's just Still' and dismissed it in polite contempt. They had seen the decline in the attendance and thought that I was going off the boil and that I could not last.

Dwindling attendances during those early years were a great source of concern to many although I was glad that increasingly I had the backing of a growing nucleus of responsive people. One of our chief officebearers was constantly nagging me about the drop in numbers until he finally left us himself.

Yet the amazing thing about it was that as our congregation became smaller, the givings each week rose. Our Treasurer often voiced his bafflement: 'Where's the money coming from?' he would ask. There was only one answer. It was given by those who had been touched by the Word.

This man was one whom I have grown to love over the years and he is one who has remained faithful even when I am sure he disliked and detested what I preached and the way things were going on in his church. For he had been here from the beginning and was in fact the major force behind me arriving in Gilcomston at all. Yet to begin with it was hard to see eye to eye, especially when his only positive comment on a service would be when I had employed a particularly graphic illustration: it was 'a good show', he would say. Later, however, I discovered that this man had resisted the Presbytery on two occasions when they would have closed Gilcomston down. Twice there had been an almighty fight about it as the church was hopelessly run down and in debt, yet he fought men like Charles T. Cox, the most formidable ecclesiastic in Scotland, to keep Gilcomston going.

And why? The reason he fought like a tiger over the church was that on the battlefield in the First World War he had called to God as he had faced death. As men fell all around him he had called to God and said, 'If you will spare my life, I'll serve your church to my dying day.' God had heard that prayer and this man had proved that it had come from the heart by his steadfast support and tenacity ever since. And I had wondered in those early days whether he was converted at all! (There weren't many converted at all in the church then although I found one or two.) For many years I was to work in fellowship of the very closest with him. I remember some years ago greeting him on a Sunday not long before a Crieff conference. I put my arms around him and said, 'My dear man, you don't know what you started all those years ago.'   'No,' he answered, 'I don't. But I see some of it and you'll come and tell me all about the conference, won't you, when you get back?'

If only all such differences could be settled so amicably! Yet when it came to the various organisations in the church which had existed for years and which as a group resisted the

Word, nothing would do but to face them head on. This was always a painful duty and was particularly so in the cases of the Women's Guild and the Boys Brigade. Again I was called up before a Presbytery committee over the Women's Guild but as they held mostly missionary meetings we suggested that it was a shame that the men could not attend them too! That was the end of the Women's Guild and the distraction it had become to the work and their attempt, it seemed, to take over the running of the church!

The matter of the Boys Brigade was not so easily settled for although the problem was of a similar nature it was more serious. It came out that the officers were speaking against the ministry and even discouraging the boys from coming to church. It was a very painful time but I knew that something had to be done to root out that evil. It was certainly incongruous that they should be using and abusing our halls and yet not be contributing anything to the work of the Gospel: much worse, they were positively antagonistic to it and to me.

Eventually I had to confront them and after much prayer I decided to take George Philip with me: he provided moral support and he was also closer in age to a number of those there. I said they could no longer use our hall which virtually meant their disbandment. The repercussions of this decision continued for a long time and yet I have never regretted it for it was one of those situations where things could not go on as they were. Something had to be done before the animosity spread and threatened to destroy the work. It was God who gave us the victory, although not without the greatest pain and humiliation to anyone with any sensitivity at all, discussed and disparaged by some of our own members and arraigned yet again before pompous ecclesiastics.

The costliness of having to deal with people in these ways - people you have known for years and have learned to love

- these are some of the trials, indeed the deaths which the minister of the Word is called to die. It requires courage but every evil that plagues, or is likely to plague the congregation or the parish must be dealt with, one way or another. First it must be taken to the throne of grace, privately, of course. Then in the Lord's own time he will lead us to deal with it. It may be that he will keep the mouth shut for ages, but tackling these issues must be in the Lord's hands if any good is to come out of them at all to produce godly and lasting growth in the fellowship.

What I would have done during these days if I had not had the prayers of Christians folk in the church behind me! Indeed there was one at least who had prayed for my coming to Aberdeen. I had only been in Gilcomston a few months when an old lady sent for me. Her name was Mrs. Fullerton and she was a member of the Baptist church in Union Grove. When I encountered her on her doorstep I thought what a wee craitur she was, an elderly lady even then, leaning heavily on a stick. When I told her my name, however, she shot out her hand to me to welcome me in: 'Come away,' she cried. 'If all I hear of you is true, you're the man a little out of the usual I've been praying for for years!'

Once we were inside she began to tell me about herself. It seemed that in years gone by she had had a Bible class of over one hundred girls. Many have since gone to the mission field but as she had grown older and more frail (she was by then in her eighties and had been a widow for seventeen years) she had become able only to sit by her fireside and pray. It was then she told me, that the Lord spoke to her and placed this burden on her heart: 'You have served me long with these girls in your local church, but this is to be the task of your life, reserved for you in your eighties - you have to pray for something in Aberdeen.'

With the prayers of good, faithful people like Mrs. Fullerton behind me and the dogged perseverance of men like my Treasurer preparing for my coming, it was with much encouragement that I faced these hard times of opposition and controversy. (I always felt it was the greatest shame that these two whom the Lord had so clearly used never met.) Having found my life's work in the weekly exposition of Scripture and seeing souls being built up in the likeness of Christ it was possible to continue, especially with the support and fellowship of a growing number in the church who either professed faith in Christ through the ministry or who joined us from time to time from other churches, craving the solid food of the Gospel.

* * * * * *

A good deal could be said about the history of consecutive Bible teaching, and my friend James Philip has gone into this more than I. It is astonishing, however how small a part such teaching has played in the total history of Christendom. The early Fathers were obviously engaged in it, but there is little sign of its continuance until the Reformation with Luther and Calvin. Most surprising of all is the fact that practically none of the 17th century Puritans favoured consecutive Bible exposition, relying on their textual preaching to cover the whole area of Scripture with, it must be admitted, a depth and thoroughness not equalled by the Reformers. Since then, even in the most spiritually prosperous days of Scotland, there is little sign of such patterns. In our day Dr. Martin Lloyd-Jones was beginning to undertake this form of Bible teaching but as I have said, I was blissfully unaware of any such parallel.

Whether I was aware of historical backing, or the lack of it or not, what I am sure about is, that the intention to consecutively minister the whole Word of God, book by book, chapter by chapter, verse by verse never left me. It began largely by accident but grew with a clear sense of mission that I must proclaim God's Word - in its entirety. Many years after that beginning when on computation I considered I had covered the whole of the Scriptures, as in sermons and mid-week Bible studies, so in Daily Bible Reading Notes, I recall the nature of the satisfaction I had. Not that I thought I had accomplished anything wonderful, since much of that ministry must have been shallow and misconceived - there was so much to learn - but that at least I had made a start. I then began to wonder how often I might cover the Scriptures after that in a lifetime, and how far I would come to understand them in order to minister to the evangelising and building-up of souls.

Yet there were times during and long after the transition when I was greatly dissatisfied with my preaching. I have very few records or copies of sermons from that time for the simple reason that some time in the late 1950s I became so dissatisfied with my ministry that in a moment of near despair I gathered every sermon note I had up to that time and destroyed them. I just threw them in the fire. Indeed, long before that in the late 1940s I can recall frequently coming home from church, and the first thing I did was to open my Bible, take out my notes and consign them to the flames and say: 'Better next time!' I recollect my Aunt remonstrating with me and saying, 'You could build on these, later, with your many references;' but I was heedless. (And the day did come, of course, when I would have been glad of those references, which had to be laboriously culled again from the Scriptures.)

However, poor as is my memory on many of these things, and scant and even non-existent as are the records, I can never forget the thrill of turning from the burdensome search for individual texts and passages for each service to the regular discipline of preaching and teaching the Word systematically. However, it was not only my own attitude to the radical change which remains with me, but the effect the systematic teaching had upon the congregation. After all, the reading of a serial story on radio or television, even in the school class-room holds interest, and what more than modern so-called 'soap operas' and long-standing series tells us that there is a value in continuity and the expectation of what the next episode will reveal which one never has in singular events and unsequential narratives?

I believe that along with prayer, consecutive ministry has contributed the most to the up-building of the Christian characters of so many whom the Lord has sent out into his work, and who after years have returned to express gratitude for the systematic teaching of the Word.

It is one thing to aim at a balanced view of Scripture, but another to provide over a period of years a balanced diet of Old Testament and New Testament and the different parts of each. There is no perfect way to do this. Doubtless a young man commencing a ministry takes stock of where he thinks his congregation, or the generality of them are, spiritually, and seeks to accommodate his ministry to their needs. In many places that will mean initially a presentation of the primary elements of the Gospel, and it may be some time before a series on any book is undertaken. Some have started series too early to an unsuspecting congregation and have bewildered the people unnecessarily and, alas, put them off the idea. In most situations one has to ease people into what may be the very new idea of serial ministry.

To preserve balance, the aim is to alternate Old and New Testaments on Sunday mornings and evenings, and try not to overlap series so that at one time one is overbalanced by one

Testament or the other. This is not easy since the volume of the Old Testament is so much greater than the New. The sequence one commences and continues will depend entirely on where the pastor thinks the people are, or what he considers they need next in their biblical education and onward spiritual progress.

It was one thing to make a stab at sequential Bible teaching and cover a few obvious books initially, but to continue into less known portions of the Word quite another. I recall how long I dreaded the day when I would have to tackle Leviticus, and Proverbs, and Revelation!

Generally speaking if a book is chosen from the Pentateuch (the first five books of the Old Testament), the next choice would be from a book on, say Psalms or the Prophets, followed by one of the historical books - Samuel, Kings or Chronicles. I kept off Proverbs for many years because I didn't know how to handle it - one verse per Sunday would have taken a lifetime! - until at last, essaying a chapter per mid-week evening the people simply hungered for its practical truths and attendances became larger than normal.

With larger books such as the Pentateuchal or the historical or prophetic books, or with a Gospel or the Acts, one found that a series of twenty to twenty-five sermons or studies was enough, and for some congregations too much. The Acts I generally divided into three so closely packed were its chapters, and prophetic books like Isaiah, Jeremiah or even Ezekiel needed to be broken up and resumed later.

Talking of Jeremiah, when it came time for that book to be considered, I feared that a weekly diet of its prophetic denunciations would pall, and so I decided to alternate the Jeremiah studies weekly with a New Testament book such as Philippians then James, and since this proved helpful, I later embarked on two sets of alternating studies: John's Gospel one Sunday morning and Isaiah (40-66) the next, with the post-exilic prophecies, Haggai, Zechariah and Malachi one Sunday evening and various short books like 2 and 3 John and Jude the other Sunday evenings.

I used to think in my ignorance, and perhaps in my fear of tackling certain portions of the Scriptures, that some of these books were possibly less than necessary, but when at last I succeeded in preaching through the whole Bible, I could recall no book so lacking in distinctiveness that to omit it from the ministry would have been a real loss to the building of Christian character.

However, to return to length of series, while twenty to twenty-five studies are generally long enough in one area of Scripture, on the other hand one has gone through whole long books - even 1 & 2 Chronicles at one go, because after hard going with the initial chapters of 1 Chronicles with its lists of names (which have their own fascination if adequately re-searched), the interest in the continuity of the historical narrative from 1 to 2 was remarkably sustained.

One of the things - the most fundamental thing really - which I have discovered in the process of systematically preaching is that there is no part of the Word of God which (although it may incur opposition and offence) when it is handled with care, respect and due attention to context and watered by prayer, does not yield saving as well as sanctifying truth.

> The Spirit breathes upon the Word
> And brings the truth to sight;
> Precepts and promises afford
> A sanctifying light.

A glory gilds the sacred page,
Majestic like the sun:
It gives a light to every age;
It gives, but borrows none.

The hand that gave it still supplies
The gracious light and heat;
His truths upon the nations rise;
They rise, but never set.

Let everlasting thanks be Thine,
For such a bright display
As makes a world of darkness shine
With beams of heavenly day.

My souls rejoices to pursue
The steps of Him I love,
Till glory breaks upon my view
In brighter worlds above.

                              William Cowper.

CHAPTER 12

THE MINISTER OF THE WORD

The role of the minister is primarily that of being the feeder of souls by means of the Word of God which is the soul's nourishment and life. It perhaps sounds a simple task put like that, yet it involves the totality of a minister's life: it is all inclusive. For if the Word is Spirit and life (John 6:63) then it must be made evident in our lives as well as in our ministries. It starts with us.

Before we can become Christ to others, by living the life and ministering the Word, we must become Christ ourselves. I mean that we must learn to live with our indwelling Saviour comfortably, happily and consistently, even if painfully. For if Christ, as far as we are concerned is only a cloak, or a robe which we put on when on duty but is not a life that we live with him in all the ordinariness of our daily lives (and ordinariness, let us not doubt, is something which Jesus loves very much) then something is far wrong. People will immediately see that and sense that the cloak does not quite fit and is sometimes discarded. In our public reading of the Word, for example, at best they will separate us from Christ and choose him: at worst, they may reject him as not having the ability to conquer and possess the preacher. They will assume that Christ is not worth having because he is not able to do a satisfactory work in or for the preacher. They will therefore turn away from the Lord, regarding him as but an empty name.

Now I will discuss pulpit style in subsequent chapters but when some allowance is made for seemly behaviour in public, such as audibility and proper presence, the whole matter of pulpit style seems to be a matter of becoming one's true self in Jesus Christ. For any man to project a true image of Jesus Christ, the real Jesus, not pietised or sanctimonised, it has to be the image of Jesus shining through him - his flesh, his human nature, no one else's. All of this is elementary, but like so many elementary or rudimentary things it is too easily forgotten because we tend to be forever straining for the abstruse and the impressive, even the far-fetched, and certainly the new. We forget that the new is old and the old is new, when and where Jesus is involved.

Yet the Word is 'made flesh' so little in our lives and in our ministries! Why is this? I believe it is because the Word has not yet become fully flesh in *us*, not having worked itself through into our flesh either for us to become glowing witnesses for Christ, living the life amongst men, or (and there must be a close connection) as ministers ministering the Word effectually in preaching and teaching and in pastoral work. If this is so it can only be because our own carnal flesh is conflicting and competing with what one can only call, the flesh of Christ within us. There is an unforgettable verse which I always think of in connection with this: 'Except a corn of wheat fall into the ground and die, it abides alone. But if it dies it bears much fruit.' (John 12:24) This text simplifies things wonderfully. What we have not yet done is to die radically and experimentally enough for Christ and his glorious purposes for others through us to get an effectual 'innings' in our lives and in our service.

Think of Peter. I doubt if even Pentecost could have done anything for Peter if he had not gone out and wept bitterly after he denied his Lord when, as you remember, his eye caught his

Master's all-searching look. That was necessary. Peter had to die then.

The deaths one dies before ministry can be of long duration - it can be hours and days before we minister, before the resurrection experience of anointed preaching. And then there is another death afterwards, sometimes worse than the death before. From the moment that you stand there dead in Christ and dead to everything you are and have and ever shall be and have, every breath you breathe thereafter, every thought you think, every word you say and deed you do, must be done over the top of your own corpse or reaching over it in your preaching to others. Then it can only be Jesus that comes over and no one else. And I believe that every preacher must bear the mark of that death. Your life must be signed by the Cross, not just Christ's Cross (there is really no other) but your cross in his Cross, your particular and unique cross that no one ever died - the cross that no one ever could die but you and you alone: your death in Christ's death.

When I came to Gilcomston, that was all deaths and reconsecrations as I have sought to show in the events of those early years, and life has been one long reconsecration with many deaths ever since. All the great pleasure of my present life and all that I enjoy - for life is fuller and richer and sweeter than it has ever been for me - has constantly come out of what has seemed to my human spirit to be rotten, dunged death. Each time I had to come back to that point I reached as a laddie of thirteen with the same feeling and call I knew then for the first time to cast myself utterly upon the Lord.

I did not know then anything about being united with Christ in his death and resurrection. I thought it was something that only I could do, although now I know that it was Christ already in me bringing me to that inevitable point. All I knew then was that I had to die to self as well as to sin.

Somehow or other that became clear to me, that I had to die to self just as really as if I had given myself over to mortal death. It was as clear and distinct as that. It was the Lord who came and stood beside me and said not just in mere words but in something deeper than words, 'Die, son. Yes, die. Cease to be. This is the end. Hand your life over to me.' Nevertheless, as I feel I have often preached too much, it was only the negative side of that that I saw then because I must confess that I thought the Lord was very cruel in that he seemed to offer me nothing, just 'Come and die. Life with its treasures, hopes and ambitions,' he seemed to say, 'is over for you forever.' In subsequent years when I pursued a life immersed in music I tried to escape this demand but it could not be dodged.

It reminds me of the play 'Hassan'. There is a line in that which recurs and recurs. In the end the character is being carried down the stream and these words keeps coming into his mind. They say that people think furiously when they are drowning and the character cannot prevent the repetition of this line burning into his mind: 'The flowers are not for you to pick, the flowers are not for you to pick.' That is exactly what I felt the Lord was saying to me.

That 'coming to an end of oneself' is a painful process but it is something the minister must know something about. I do not mean in the petulant sense of being all incensed at your own ineptitude, for that kind of unwilling skirmish with death only breeds a more determined self-effort: we will try harder next time, determined to live at all costs. Instead it is the point where you have been brought broken-heartedly to where you have begun to see the greatness of Christ which fills not only your horizon, but your heart and life and thought and your all. You have been standing before him, perhaps unwittingly, as a tiny obstacle to his great and holy will and he comes and confronts you and commands you to bow to that will and give yourself utterly to him. Such an experience is probably like that of Saul of Tarsus at his conversion on the Damascus road, however it may happen to you.

However it happens, it is an unforgettable experience and if it is really of God it will last for the rest of your life. I can instantly feel what I felt at thirteen and again at seventeen when God called me back to himself as I sat broken-hearted at my organ in the Methodist Church that night. Subsequently you may slip away from it a thousand times as alas we all do, but once you have been marked inwardly and branded by the sign of Christ's Cross, pricked indelibly by the sharp needle of his Spirit on your heart, then you will bear that mark forever.

It is interesting about marks. I have a great mark across the front of my forefinger which was made after I was taken away from Gordon's College at thirteen on account of ill-health, having been there only three weeks. I was sent away to a farm in Tarland in Aberdeen-shire until Christmas to try to recover and as I was busy one day in the fields topping and tailing the turnips I nearly topped and tailed my finger with the curved 'heuk' as the knife was called. That mark is there as clear as can be today. It is indelible in me. Whether or not it will be glorified like the Lord's wounds which, as the hymn writer says in that wonderful part of *Crown him with many crowns*, will be 'in beauty glorified', I don't know. I will have a look some day when we are 'upstairs' walking the golden streets!

But surely that is what Paul meant when he said he bore the marks of Jesus Christ 'indelibly' or as Toplady says in his hymn, 'the marks of indelible grace'. They are surely in us to stay because they are eternally branded in us by him. Let me say that even the metaphor of marks or brands is too superficial, just as a needle is not enough although it gives the idea of penetration. For we must be careful that it is not the idea of pain that is predominant and not the pain that we look for to verify the experience.

I can recall times when my death in Jesus has seemed to call me to the most painful exploits, not only humiliating but going against the grain. One occasion cannot be forgotten when as a young man of about seventeen I astonished the whole family as we sat around the tea table on a Sunday evening by blurting out that we were going to pray. To everyone's embarrassment, especially my father's, I lurched into the most awkward prayer you have ever heard. I never did it again. It was a disaster but I did it because I believed God was daring me to do it and it was such a painful experience that I concluded that it must be from him. Was it? I don't know but I don't think so.

As a complete contrast to that, the broken-hearted, melting sensation deep down in our hearts that we should seek should be found when we are faced with Jesus dying for us on the Cross. It is following on from that that we yield ourselves utterly to him and do his bidding with joy and it is this which brings a sensation of the most incredible sweetness. The painfulness is not what is important. We could even call it, as Shakespeare does, 'bitter sweet', although the sweetness is so intense that it is actually excruciating. It is like the man who heard Beethoven for the first time and who said it was so beautiful he could scarcely bear it.

This sweetness in the midst of self-immolation, comes only from the fact that we are never bearing our hurt and pain alone. There is no aloneness here. I think it has taken most of my life to realise this and learn it, that any desolation I feel which brings a sense of utter forsakenness is not of God at all. It is to be refused because Jesus never leaves us quite alone. He may avert his face and withdraw the conscious, felt sense of his presence from us for a time when we sin, but that is a

different experience from dying in the sense that I mean here.
It brings to mind the hymn of John Ellerton's which says,

> Lord, should fear and anguish roll
> Darkly o'er my sinful soul,
> Thou, who once wast thus bereft
> That thine own might ne'er be left,
> Teach me by that bitter cry
> In the gloom to know thee nigh.

That's it! He went through all that alone so he might lead
us safely through it, never alone. In the last two lines of the
Passion Chorale, Paul Gerhardt says, 'For he who dies
believing, dies safely'. Although it is the finality of mortal
death that Gerhardt is speaking of there, this experience which
I am trying to describe is so close to it that it has all the similar
'burn your boats' or 'bridges' feeling of finality about it. This
is, I believe, perfectly right for us to apply to our mortification
in the moral and spiritual sense.

In the light of many things which happened in Gilcomston
in those early days, unpleasantnesses which were hard to
endure, it seems to me that there is one quality which a
minister of the Word must possess to be fruitful. Along with
Solzhenitsyn who spoke of this theme in his famous Harvard
speech, I would say that this quality is courage: guts, sheer
lion-hearted bravery, clarity of mind and purpose, grit. Weaklings are no use here. They have a place in the economy of God
if they are not deliberate weaklings and stunted adults as Paul
writes of both to the Romans and to the Corinthians. But
weaklings are no use to go out and speak prophetically to men
from God and declare with all compassion, as well as with
faithfulness, the truth: the divine Word that cuts across all
men's worldly plans for their own lives.

That may mean unexpected things. One aim you ought to have is to build self-perpetuating ministries which will last generations. Deuteronomy 7:9 says that the Word of God is going to go on to a thousand generations. Do we take that seriously? That may mean that in addition to drawing many to hear the Word of truth, many may be immediately, or almost immediately be driven by the Lord beyond your parish. You will lose your best people, although we should not use the word 'lose' even of those who go far across the seas.

But it may mean other things and you must learn to apply the Word to the situation in which you find yourself. That will mean that you have to apply the Word to evils rampant and prevailing in your midst: some open, some hidden. You will have to rebuke evil. Indeed, it is one of the commands issued at the ordination service for ruling elders as well as for teaching elders, ministers of the Word: 'Show yourself zealous to promote virtue: not to fear the faces of the wicked, but to rebuke their wickedness.'

* * * * * *

But there are certain pre-requisites: one of the most important is that the minister needs the assurance that he is where he is in God's will. Don't get up and say, 'I must move!' unless God says so. I see God working against dear men who want to move, and he won't let them. He is saying, 'Stay where you are and fight it out and win through!' I would say that the one thing, beyond the fundamental things, that has kept me in that box for forty-six years, and I hope will keep me for another ten, is what I have said hundreds of times: 'God took me by the scruff of the neck and here I stand. Men can go mad if they like but only God will budge me.'

There was a time, near the end of 1965, when I began to feel that my time at Gilcomston would soon be over. Something new was needed, I felt, and I was increasingly dissatisfied with my own ministry. It was as if, in the course of edifying our people over a number of years the pendulum had swung too far and it was necessary now to swing back again. What was needed, I realised, was a new evangelistic drive.

Yet I did not feel fit to bring about this change. For some time - I was now in my fifties - I had suffered periods of exhaustion. Occasionally I would need suddenly to have a Sunday off and would have to call someone to take the pulpit at short notice. In combination with this physical weariness I felt a certain woolliness in my thought patterns. Never a particularly rational creature, it was as if there was now a cloud over me under which I struggled to persevere.

It had been in May of that year that the congregation had generously presented me with a holiday in Israel. This had been a new experience for me, going abroad and it had a jangling effect on me spiritually. I do not know the actual cause, whether it was due simply to tiredness or whether the religious paganism I saw affected me, but I felt jaded and found it hard on my return to gather the threads of my ministry together again.

Was I to leave Gilcomston therefore? After twenty years of me did they need someone new? It was only as 1966 began that I realised, yes, Gilcomston needed a new man and I could not ignore God's voice any longer: 'You!' he was saying. 'You are to be that new man.'

That was a turning point. It ushered in a new phase in the ministry and in particular, in the preaching. For we moved dramatically to shorter, more evangelistic services. Instead of a two hour service, it sometimes was as short as forty-five minutes! It was a time of outreach when our young folk ran a Coffee Bar, first with the Salvation Army and then on their own. This was a rowdy affair with amplified music, guitars -

even flashing lights! That went on for about two years before the need again arose for more regular teaching from the Word. But it met a specific need as I was concerned that we were becoming complacent and forgetful of the unsaved and needed to focus our attention particularly on reaching out beyond ourselves. Since that time I have never again felt such unsettledness, nor the befuddled feeling in my brain. This seemed to lift and I now have what I feel is greater clarity than ever, and as I have said, no intimation or inclination to retire.

Another pre-requisite for the minister is the authority of the Holy Spirit and the assurance that the Holy Spirit will not desert you in doing your duty. To me it is all a matter of seeking to do a local job faithfully before God. Indeed, this is very important in view of the Word spreading wider as people may come from across the border and over the seas having heard about the work and work like it in other places. If your work happens to have wider repercussions as some work seems to have, then leave that in God's hands and nobody else's. Try to ignore it as much as possible for in a sense it is none of your business.

I am always happiest and most satisfied when I see myself, whatever other people may say or do, as the minister of our own little church here in Aberdeen. It has always been a help to me at the mundane level to see myself as called by God but paid by the congregation to do this job. The first thing is to preach. If I did not do this job, whatever other job in the world I might do, I would be failing in my contract both to God and to the people of Gilcomston. There is nothing higher in the whole world than to be a faithful parish or pastoral minister. If you are a national or even a regional figure you can get away with a lot: you can hide when you like. But if you are committed to one community, wherever it may be, you have to measure up to it or be found wanting. And if you are found wanting than everyone knows it and your witness is mud.

There is a well known hymn which says, 'Each victory will help you some other to win'. In one sense the various deaths that you may be called to die will not only lead to their inevitable resurrections, but each will enable you to die another death that there may be another resurrection. When you have gone through a gruelling test at school or college, the reward is a harder test to come, isn't it? That's true of life. Each death and resurrection will lead to another, if not immediately then later. And if the resurrections are not seen on earth in respect of deaths you have died and forgotten all about, what joy there will be in heaven to discover these jewels you never knew you possessed! That is what I partly take reward in heaven to mean. Then we will know. What a comfort this is! We will know that there was never a death, however painful, which was not fruitful to the Lord, for resurrection must follow death in the Lord. Yet the signs here and now will be seen in the life of the church as the minister plumbs the depths. The fruit will begin to show as the people feed on the Word and as it passes through his crucified life into theirs.

CHAPTER 13

THE CONDUCT OF PUBLIC WORSHIP

The experience of years of conducting public worship teaches many things: bearing, deportment, manner of speech, all of which should reflect the simplicity of Christ, and inspire worshippers to devote themselves to the worship of God with joyful seriousness. It is shameful that so little time and study is given to these things when they can assist so powerfully in, or equally detract from the worship. It is important for these practicalities to be taken seriously. They are vital in showing the whole service as worship to God and as such each part, from the opening greeting to the Benediction, must be conducted in a worthy manner. The minister's approach to the sacred task from the moment he enters the church should be one of humble dignity and reverence, without exaggeration of behaviour of any kind.

I have found it helpful while reverent music is played to enter the church as people are gathering, and to move round discreetly and quietly greeting those involved in the service: the organist, the recorder in the recording room, the officebearers at the door, the little ones coming in with their teachers, and any in particular who may be visiting or re-visiting us. Then I make my way to the Communion Table for the commencement of the service. Such an entry tends to narrow any gap that is imagined between minister and people, and shows that he is but one of themselves appointed to his

particular task. A 'Good Morning' greeting to the congregation leads to a simple call to worship, 'Let us worship God'.

A word needs to be said here about what in the histrionic
world is called 'timing'. The aim of all who seek to capture
and hold the attention of audiences is to maintain interest and
prevent minds wandering. To that end, in the worship of
Almighty God, no pauses, however reverently intended, or
gaps in proceedings should be permitted whatsoever. As soon
as the organ music ceases the minister should be on his feet
announcing the worship in an eager voice calculated to
encourage people to sing from their hearts. Any impression
of delay, hesitancy, uncertainty or even weariness or boredom
is calculated to put people off and lose their interest almost
before the service has started. (A pregnant pause, such as in
prayer, or preaching is a very different thing!)

The psalm or hymn is then announced and repeated in a
clear voice giving the place and number, reading a line or two,
possibly naming the tune to be sung, and any observation on
the choice in relation to the theme of the service.

The authors of hymns should interest congregations, although reference to them should not be overdone, but if the
hymn is old, the approximate date may be given, or if the
writer belongs to a particular age or denomination. This helps
intelligent participation, and it is astonishing how little it is
done. There need be no intrusion into the solemnities of
worship by such helpful comments, since our God is no tyrant
or stickler for mere etiquettes, but is our gracious heavenly
Father who wants us to approach his worship with natural
humility and eager reverence and keenness.

Prayer which follows may be introduced by some call to
approach the Lord and some contemplation of whom we are
approaching. This is especially helpful when the atmosphere
is not particularly conducive to worship; and since prayer is

one of the most important parts of worship, it should never be hurried, but time should be taken to lead the people into the presence of God and there remain in contemplation of his Majesty until hearts are subdued and drawn nearer to him. If the Lord's Prayer is repeated, it should be said far more slowly than most people gabble it.

The reading of Holy Scripture is perhaps the most important part of worship, for everything flows from God's holy Word. The place of the reading should be announced clearly, giving people time to find it in their Bibles. If introduction is necessary it should be thought out and given in the fewest possible words and the Word read with all due sense, but without exaggerated characterisation. It seems that for some time I was known for my Bible readings - or so I am told - and if this is so it is because I believe in giving due time and consideration to the reading of the Word. Often larger sections need to be read to give the sense, and explanations may have to be given throughout. I hope that I do not interrupt the flow; for to read in an informed way and therefore for the hearers to likewise attend in an informed way is surely better than to gabble through a passage in an uninteresting or easily ignored monotone as if to say, 'Well, we know all that.'

I fear that many ministers even of years of experience seem to regard the reading of Holy Scripture as a kind of necessary preliminary; but if the reading is preliminary to the preaching, it is vastly more important than the preaching, for it alone is the pure Word to which the minister's preaching must seek to be faithful. The minister ought to live the passage he is reading, so that every nuance of its truth comes forth clearly and plainly. It is a poor reader of Holy Writ who does not find an authority in declaring the Word which may far outweigh the sense of power and liberty he may enjoy in the subsequent preaching.

There was a time when I was more dramatic in the pulpit than I am now - I mean in physical movement. So excited would I get that I used to stride about and even hung from the pillars. I often felt too that imaginative movement helped the congregation to grasp what are really visual images, such as to dramatise the piercing of the Saviour's hands.

But those were the days when I went into the pulpit with ideas and some notes rather than actual word for word scripts as I use nowadays in my preaching and this change came about really because it seemed that it was becoming harder to follow my lines of thought, sometimes even for me! I remember one instance when, having digressed from my point I couldn't find my way back into the sermon. Hitting my forehead with my hand in bewilderment I admitted that I could not remember where I was. I was informed later that a dear friend in the gallery whispered, 'Serves you right!'

So the digressions had to be controlled - although some have told me that it was through a particular aside that they were converted - and I began to use a full manuscript, thus effectively pinning me to the spot. I type this script out during the week and spend Friday and Saturday reading and reread-ing it to impress its substance on my mind. I also mark the text to indicate emphasis or inflexions in the voice in an attempt to maintain interest while I read. It has been a concern of mine that I now have very little eye contact with the congregation which is so important but I think it is unfortunately one of the preaching tools that I have had to forego. This is certainly not ideal.

I did try using a manuscript many years before when George Philip harangued me after a sermon for being 'all over the place' and to 'stop rambling'. Yet when I tested this out in following weeks, he suggested I forget what he had said and revert to how I had been before! 'Throw away the notes,' he said. 'It's too flat.' Now that I do use a script I hope that I have learned how to adjust to some of its disadvantages, and use the inflexions of the voice to arrest attention rather than relying on the visual. Eargate is more important than Eyegate!

As far as speaking to little children is concerned, the aim should be to give them a message worthy of their young minds but with adjustments for age without diminution of content, for they also are the church, within the one covenant of grace. The last thing in the world one must do is to speak down to children: they may within their little minds be the most intelligent and responsive part of the congregation!

Other parts of the service, such as the receiving of the people's offerings must be done with due solemnity, with dedication of the givers before the gifts, that the gifts may be acceptable to a holy God. In our own practice, dedication leads to intercession for Christ's church in the world and for her impact upon it as a lost world, with prayers for those in special need and in authority, and reference to events in the world which are the responsibility of the church to pray for. Then the Holy Spirit needs to be invoked for the preaching of the Word.

There is excellent instruction on preaching in Paul's letter to the Romans (10:14,15). What the Good News is has been declared in the previous verses concerning 'Jesus as Lord' that 'Everyone who calls on the name of the Lord will be saved'. But preachers have to be sent - all Christians are not called to preach which is different from witnessing, to which every believer is called: 'Let your light so shine before men, that they may see your good works, and glorify your Father who is in heaven'. Paul continues: 'How beautiful are the feet of those who bring good news'. Yes, but how are they to declare the Good News so that people will listen and believe?

It is an old objection, but I fear still relevant, that while the actor declares his theatrical fictions as if they were Gospel truth and makes people listen; the preacher often speaks the Good News of the Gospel as if it were not very important and not particularly to be heeded. There seems to be a kind of belief even among certain types of devout preachers that having spoken the good words, however they are muttered or intoned, they have fulfilled their duty, and it is up to men to heed the words, however spoken. There is a fatalism about such a view which ill accords with the importance of the Good News.

If the Good News of the Gospel in the Word of God is the greatest and most important News in the world, then no trouble should be spared in declaring it, that men may hear it well, and heed it with all their hearts. And although this may be a digression, the same applies to those who essay to speak to God in corporate prayer. There is a kind of devotion quite misplaced and misdirected which thinks because one is addressing Almighty God, an attitude of abasement must include a form of bated-breath muttering which can be either difficult to hear and follow or sometimes quite incoherent. Alas such devout persons if charged with muttering incomprehensibly, might reply, 'But I am not praying to you, but to God.' Yes, but prayers in a corporate fellowship are meant to be heard, so that the saints may respond with hearty 'Amens' that the prayers be answered. How can we say 'Amen' to a prayer we have not heard. It might be something we disagree with!

But to preachers. The voice must be raised. Everyone knows that in an urgent situation such as a house on fire, a muttered warning will not summon and alert either those in danger or the fire-fighters. One must learn to raise one's voice in preaching as in corporate prayer. Until one has done so, one ought not to be preaching. But the preacher has to learn, you say. Yes, but some experience in corporate prayer can help that, and to those with a potential gift, the adjustment of raising the voice should come almost naturally.

To give an example, I was longing recently to hear a certain young man take part in prayer wondering whether there was, as I suspected, a preaching gift although the voice was soft and somewhat inturned, I was astonished when the voice was eventually raised in prayer to find it resonant and quite commanding, and the prayer fluent. This at once confirmed what I had heard of this young man's call to the ministry. Indeed, it is often in corporate prayer that one has the first intimation that a youngster has a preaching gift, because the voice is suitably raised and the fluency of the expression affords evidence of the potential.

On the other hand, there are those apparently called to the ministry who after years, do not seem to break free from preoccupation with inturned self, and who therefore fail to become real heralds. The first qualification of a town-crier is to be able to shout! There is no need to shout in preaching, but one has not only to be heard, but one must command attention. It is this lack of command which makes one wonder whether some men are really called to the ministry. They do not make people sit up and take notice. All that can be said of them is that the Word is spoken in people's hearing. If there is a natural shyness or reticence which forbids the speaker raising his voice commandingly without drawing undue attention to himself, then the impression left is either that the preacher is not sure about what he is saying or else he is not paying sufficient attention to the presentation of it. Especially in these days when recorders are as common as telephones, there is no excuse for a potential and aspiring preacher not listening to his efforts and profiting from what will very likely be a humiliating experience! Surely part of the proof of a call to the ministry is that there is a natural gift in evidence, and the seemly raising of the voice is one of the ways that it may be recognised.

But it is not only a question of raising the voice, but of articulating one's speech. There are some speakers whose articulation is so bad that the voice sounds like a booming noise in the ears - all vowels and no consonants! The apostle Paul speaks about this to the Corinthians when he says, 'Even in the case of lifeless things that make sounds, such as the flute or the harp, how will anyone know what tune is being played unless there is a distinction in the notes? Again, if the trumpet does not sound a clear call, who will get ready for the battle? So it is with you. Unless you speak intelligible words with your tongue, how will anyone know what you are saying? You will just be speaking into the air.'

The truth is that many who are apparently called to the ministry still need a thorough course in elocution. There is not only the matter of volume, and articulation, but pitch and modulation. While sufficient tone must be produced, that does not mean that a pitch is set as a permanency as in cathedrals where it is wrongly believed that only a voice sustaining the pitch on one note can be heard throughout the echoing building - a great mistake. Nothing in the world could be more artificial than a bleating voice sounding one note perpetually as if the speaker were in pain. Maybe he is: his hearers certainly are, if they have any concept of humble naturalness in approaching the throne of grace. It is perfectly possible for the voice to maintain a proper volume and articulate the words clearly and still modulate the pitch in an interesting and appealing manner.

Indeed, where it is difficult to hold attention for some reason, due possibly to some distraction, or because one's material or the way it is presented has not proved particularly

arresting, this can be done by a slight exaggeration in the
modulations of the voice, especially adopting a somewhat
higher pitch. One has often found that where interest flags,
the raising the pitch of the voice commands new attention. At
the same time, it is important not to try mere elocutionary
tricks, or to assume supposedly devout forms of expression
different from one's normal and natural voice, for that is
almost always apparent to the hearers as artificial, or at least
as a striving for effect which defeats its own end. There is a
style of reading, preaching and praying which seems to let the
voice trail away at the end of sentences as if there were
something too devoutly mysterious at the end of the sentence
to be heard at all - a most aggravating habit, and far too
common.

Where the heart and mind are set on the Word and work of
God, there ought to be a quality of conviction in the declaration of the truth which speaks in matter-of-fact tones with no
histrionic tricks of voice or mannerism for mere effect. It is
sufficient that one declares the truth of God loudly and clearly
since it needs no artifice, tricks or self-conscious techniques,
only those proper techniques as handmaids to the preaching
which help to make the Word heard and heeded. How often
when a prophet, apostle or, as in the Revelation an angel in
Scripture is making a pronouncement, it is declared 'with a
loud voice'. It is this command which will make the Word of
God, watered by the tearful prayers of the saints, reach not
only people's ears, but their minds, consciences, wills and
their hearts, to their progressive transformation into the
likeness of Christ.

The end of this in every service should be such singing of
the closing praise as is a worthy offering to Almighty God for
the richness of his Truth, and for its saving practicalities.

CHAPTER 14

THE CRIEFF BROTHERHOOD

The Crieff Brotherhood is perhaps best known today for its fostering of the cause of Evangelicalism in the Church of Scotland. This, however, is more of an assumption made in some quarters rather than its original intended function. The original motivation behind what became the Brotherhood was, as is often the case with something that grows, much simpler and more innocent.

It began in the late summer of 1970 when I invited a score of minister friends to hear an interesting speaker. Geoffrey Dixon was an elder in our Gilcomston South congregation and in his profession as a psychiatrist his knowledge of the human mind and nature had often been of assistance to me in ministerial matters. His friendship and professional advice were of great value to me at a time when the expansion of our work at home and abroad was bringing before us an increasing number of needy folk, some of whose problems were more psychological than spiritual in nature. Although I believe that Jesus Christ is able to deal with every ill that besets humanity, one was willing to bow to the discernment and knowledgeable skill of one both versed in the Gospel and in the expertise of his field of study. The benefit I had received I felt should be shared with some of my brother ministers.

We met in Crieff in the manse of an old friend and colleague, Henry (Sandy) Tait. It was an informal gathering.

The lounge was full with every seat in use and we chatted a good deal and caught up on news before listening with great interest to Geoffrey. He spoke on personal counselling and being able to recognise the extent of our ability to assist, and where to turn, if more than we were able to give was required. It was an excellent time, and feeling that Geoffrey had much more that could prove helpful, some of us who attended the original meeting felt that it would be good to meet with him, say, once a month to the end of the year. We would pick his brains and discuss such matters as arose in our ministries. Geoffrey was due to leave for Australia in the New Year to begin a new job there so we felt that there was little time to waste. In the end four meetings were held that year with Geoffrey Dixon as our speaker.

Having begun, however, we found that these gatherings were enjoyed so much and were of such benefit that there was a desire to continue. It was clear that the meetings had been of such blessing, especially to men in beleaguered situations that we had touched on something which was helpful and perhaps needed, so we decided to continue to meet together at regular intervals.

It was at the next meeting after Christmas that it was decided to speak to specific subjects. These would provide the focus of our attention although affinity with each other's beliefs and concern for each other were what underpinned our association. As time has gone on suggestions have been made as to topics and speakers and it has been common practise for Sandy Tait, who became our efficient secretary, and I to consider these proposals and if suitable, then to invite someone to speak on that subject.

I have always taken the inviting of those who attend - ministers, students and laymen - into my own hands although names are often suggested to me, and in these letters of invitation I explain to the recipient the simple principles for which we stand. These principles have always been my guide as regards to the Brotherhood: (a) that we all stand absolutely upon the Word of God; (b) that we are committed to systematic biblical exposition, and (c) that we love and pray for each other. The caring aspect was a natural progression from the other two for it was the originally tiny number who were faithfully preaching the Word who were encountering opposition and who needed the support of one another.

Almost from the very beginning there has been a growth in the numbers of those invited to attend. The initial twenty or so quickly became thirty and soon a training centre in Crieff had to be hired to hold us. Before long the Hydro at Crieff was approached and we soon took over some public rooms there for our meetings. We were then able to spend more than part of one day together and early in 1973 out first overnight gathering was held. This was greatly enjoyed, not least because it gave us more time to enjoy fellowship together over meals or in walks in the grounds. Evenings after dinner were often particularly precious as we shared together and as the men could meet new faces and get to know each other better. This has been increasingly important as our numbers have gone up till the register now holds over three hundred names!

I have resisted attempts even as, or perhaps because, the Brotherhood has grown, to formulate any doctrinal basis. Some have also wanted to make the gathering more structured with committees and so on but since I see the Christian church as a family and local families rather than as battalions of soldiers, I think there can be as much efficiency in an informal setting as in a structured order.

The only criteria for responding to the invitation are laid out as I have mentioned and I make a point of only inviting men whom I believe are or are coming to be fundamental on the Word of God - we have no time for any kind of liberalism at all - and who are intent upon systematic biblical exposition, and who also love one another. We have a wider theological stance than many would suppose although one or two over the years have had their invitation withdrawn because they bore ill will against individuals or groups, or were contemptuous of us, or so despised the invitation that they never replied.

From the early days the Crieff Brotherhood has enjoyed the financial support of two ladies without whom it would have been difficult to exist, far less expand. Our benefactresses, however, have always wished to remain anonymous and I must respect their request. Suffice it to say that we are endlessly grateful for their interest and backing. As time has progressed, however, the Brotherhood has increasingly contributed to its own 'keep' as we thought that it was time that we shoulder at least part of the financial burden.

From those first meetings when first a specific subject was discussed and then it was decided that various papers should be brought before the men, a wide spectrum of topics has been presented. Many have focused on doctrine and on biblical teaching, sometimes with a historical or biographical emphasis. Thus the Brotherhood has sought to 'minister to the minister' and provide a place where he can receive and learn rather than give out and teach as he does from week to week. We are distinctly blessed in that several of our men have exceptional academic skills and we have made use of them frequently! Many papers have been published having received their airing at Crieff.

Primarily, however, Sandy Tait and I have sought to stick to the more practical emphasis with which we began. Church issues, both local and national are included and there is often discussion on General Assembly reports from year to year. Topics such as the role of children in the church, public prayer and counselling have been introduced more than once with more thorny issues like divorce and remarriage also featuring. I have often found that situations which have arisen for one minister turn out to be common dilemmas amongst others and as these come out in discussion they are often included in the agenda for a subsequent gathering. The pastoral element is therefore very strong and linked to this we have tried to ensure, either formally or informally, that reports and news of various ministries are heard. Apart from anything else these form the core of our prayers as we pray for each other during the gatherings and of course once we have all gone home.

Particular emphasis had always been given to the specific work and role of the minister. This includes all the particular stresses and priorities which are his and are those of his family in the manse. A great help in broadening this theme was the inclusion of wives and fiancees for our Ladies' Days, the first of which was held in 1975. One of our talks on the family was led, surprisingly, by William Still! I recall saying that although a bachelor I was brought up in the middle of six and therefore had something to say!

The variety in the topics discussed and in those who have presented them has meant that each Crieff gathering had been different: some are moving, some are informative, most are challenging and helpful. Differing views are sometimes expressed on one issue, such as the time some ten years ago when we had three speakers who all addressed the creation/evolution debate. It took all day, I remember and the somewhat divergent albeit conservative views were expressed in a most cordial and good-humoured spirit - an example of Christian charity.

We have often welcomed to Crieff various visitors who have addressed us. 1990 was a year which seemed to see unprecedented numbers of them as we were joined twice by transatlantic friends: first, Charles Colson of the International Prison Fellowship, and later in the year, Elisabeth Elliot, ex-missionary and author of *Through Gates of Splendour* and other books. Others who attended were three speakers who had been present at the Manila Congress for World Evangelism: Fergus MacDonald of the National Bible Society, Colin Sinclair of Scripture Union, and Bob McGhee.

Throughout each gathering we have held times of prayer together both in the morning and after particular talks. Perhaps these have been the most precious times at Crieff when we bring one another before the Lord seeking his guidance and claiming his compassion on ourselves. It is then that we come as a body of believers, a family, to his throne for the refreshment and motivation which our times at Crieff have so often been known to stimulate.

From time to time we have held some congregational singing together which I have sought to lead. We have even taped it and when I hear it I am astonished at the clarity of diction (always one of my pet subjects!) as well as by its heartiness and sonority. Every word can be heard distinctly - a lesson for musicians on what sanctification can do!

But what of the future? Now and again questions have been asked, but for all my heart-searching, and prompted by advisors from near and far that it was time to specify its future leadership, I have little or no guidance to give. I have always been willing that the Brotherhood, as all things, should cease as a group when its purpose had been served, and that is still my opinion. At times I have thought that it had outlived its usefulness because we are now so many men all over the place that no man in the ministry needs to feel that lonely, and yet, we continue. If it died with me I wouldn't mind, and maybe it will, or become something so very different that I would not own it!

Attempts have been made occasionally to turn the Crieff Brotherhood into a pressure group but these I have assiduously resisted. Whatever other people say about us, we know that its purpose is as innocently open as ever, namely to stand together upon the Word of God, affording support and fellowship to those who minister that Word systematically, and to love one another.

CHAPTER 15

MUSIC IN THE SERVICE OF THE CHURCH

I hesitate to begin discussion of this subject because music was the first love of my life until Christ took over; and there is so much to say that I am not sure how much is relevant to my life's work.

To keep to the subject, the cumulative effect of an early life involved in much music-making has been its application to the worship of the Lord's house, especially to congregational praise. Having had much experience of anthems sung by choirs in Christian worship, I somewhat reluctantly came to the conclusion that there was virtually no place for one group of Christians singing to the other (apart from antiphonal singing which is different), since praise is the privilege of the whole congregation.

Indeed, in the United Free tradition of the Church of Scotland the congregation in my recollection used to stand, many of them with their own anthem books in expectation that they would join the choir in singing the anthem. Yet eventually anthems became so specialised that it was futile for the congregation to stand since they couldn't join in. Thus the anthem became a specialised performance.

I think I was confirmed in my view on choirs in the service of the Lord when worshipping in a service conducted by Professor J. S. Stewart many years go. After some fine congregational singing, the choir sang a piece from Brahms'

Requiem immediately before Professor Stewart preached, and I recall that the non-participation of the congregation, for all the fine singing, seemed to cool the spiritual temperature considerably. Although the Professor preached well with liberty and eloquence, he had to start from cold, which didn't help. Nothing could be more inspiring to a preacher commencing his sermon than to launch out on the wings of fervent congregational praise. If a preacher couldn't preach after that, surely he couldn't preach at all!

The most important part of a minister's responsibility as far as congregational singing is concerned is to gain a knowledge of hymnody to enable him to find the right words to support the ministry of the Word. As to tunes, he needs an equal knowledge of hymn tunes and, doubtless in co-operation with the leader of praise, should know how to fit hymns to tunes so as to help expedite the message of the Word.

I have often assisted young men in this and it is amazing what a difference even a little knowledge can make. For I always ask myself some questions, such as, 'Are there too many verses of equal length or in long metre', or 'Do the tunes as well as the words reflect the tone or theme one is trying to pursue - perhaps repentance, celebration or reverence'.

Not every minister is a musician or has musical experience, but it is astonishing how much knowledge can be acquired if the minister as a lover of the Word searches the Psalter and Hymnaries for praise conducive to true worship in terms of the Word to be read and preached. This is a task calling for constant study and application, and even after many years of experience, it may almost take as long to choose items of praise and their tunes in keeping with the Word to be declared as it takes to prepare the ministry of the Word itself. Yet when a service holds together because the message is clear, the hymns support it and the congregation responds with praise from the heart, there is no more God-glorifying and satisfying experience on earth!.

It has always been my desire that the praises of the Lord's people should confirm that the congregation is far more than an audience for the preacher; and one of the most potent answers to criticism of Presbyterian worship by extreme charismatics is a congregation pouring out its soul to God in Spirit-inspired praise.

The factors which govern such an experience of God-blessed praise are various, but one of the most important is the tempo at which hymns are sung. An excellent hymn can be ruined because the tempo is either too fast or too slow, and it hardly matters whether it is the one or the other, for slowness is deadening, as hurried singing (to keep up with a racing organist) can turn the profoundest hymn into an unholy scramble calculated to evacuate the experience of all its soul-satisfying blessing.

I think that if God has given me any particular gift in a musical direction it is a sense of timing and tempo. There is a tempo for every tune according to its rhythmic and harmonic structure, although there is room for adjustment to suit different styles and themes of the hymn it is sung. English congregations tended to sing hymns at too fast a speed, as many Scottish congregations sing their psalms too slowly. An experience of Songs of Praise on television can be ruined by wrong tempo; whether it is the time factor in a programme or for other reasons, hymns are rushed through at break-neck speed. Far better to omit verses, although that may not be good for the hymn if it ought to be sung as a whole, than to rush the hymn through in a certain number of minutes to please the producer.

My musical education began with Miss Sim of Holburn Street where my sister Barbara had been a pupil. Miss Sim wanted us to sit Trinity College exams and I have certificates for several Junior ones. Of course, ill-health from the age of seven dogged me, but when I wasn't very fit for other things and was often off school with nervous trouble and the skin eruptions which went with it, I kept at the piano, until by the age of fourteen I was able to accompany singers at the Salvation Army and at mission halls. Indeed, I have recalled how Charles Dent my bandleader was singing at Craiginches prison one Sunday afternoon and would have me accompany him, but I was not quite fourteen which was the age limit for entrance to prison! I went a number of times after that when I was the age.

Encouraged in various brass instruments in the Salvation Army throughout my teens, I began to aspire to a musical career although my first loves were always the piano and organ. During the years with the Methodist Church which I have described when I was in rebellion to God, my only solace was my piano. These were the loneliest years of my life, away from friends as well as the Lord. It was just prior to this time that the Lord had indicated to me that I would remain single: I would never marry. That was the bitterest blow and music was the only means I had of expressing my anguish. Often the keys of my piano would swim with tears as I confided to that instrument, my medium of self expression, the sorrow I felt that the Lord was calling me to what I saw as a life of complete loneliness.

The four years that followed, while still music teaching were most productive of the kind of musical activity common to the Army and included a good deal of creative work, including an anthem I wrote to the words of *When I survey the wondrous Cross*. This was sung on the eve of my leaving for the International College of the Salvation Army in Denmark Hill, London to train as a Salvation Army Officer.

My nervous trouble which left me helpless for years after meant that I was practically useless for any sort of service. I was still in the Salvation Army but not doing anything. Yet it was my interest in music which began to let me become involved again. As my improvement continued and I began to feel again the Lord's hand on me to proclaim his Word, I was advised to stay where I was. I was doing a fine job, it seemed, conducting the Singers. It was more than had really been expected of me. But I knew that the Lord had called me to a higher service than this for all that music might play its part along the way!

Later that year visiting the London Musical Festival to hear Toscannini, I went with my sister to Clapton Congress Hall Salvation Army because my younger sister Rene had linked up there having come to London as a typist in the Law Courts. Albert Osborne was preaching, and he came to greet me afterwards. How was the Army in Aberdeen? 'I don't know,' I said, 'I have left it to train for the Church of Scotland ministry.' He turned and walked away without a word. Years later, meeting my sister Barbara in a corridor of the Albert Hall at some great Rally he asked about Aberdeen, and having heard of the work of Gilcomston in its early stages was rather abashed and admitted his 'mistake'. 'No mistake,' said my sister, 'my brother's in the right place and doing good work.'

Of the years of musical activity while I was a University student I have written already, and looking back now after those many years of choosing praise for the worship of God in Gilcomston, I can see how my varied musical experiences prior to 1945 (including recitals with professionals at Springburnhill Parish Church, Glasgow) helped me immeasurably to acquire judgment in these matters, and particularly with the help of such a genius as Gordon Ross as our organist for thirty-nine years to set a standard of Christian praise which has been,

I believe, an inspiration to many.

One of the greatest blessings of my ministry as a musical minister has been to have been served by two such excellent musicians as Gordon Ross and Andrew Tulloch. What I would have done if like some ministers I had been saddled with an unmusical or incompetent or uncooperative organist, I don't know!

I first heard Gordon Ross play in John Knox Gerrard Street when I preached there as a student. There was a musical fluency and a warm evangelical tone about his extemporary voluntaries which were vitally related to the hymns we were singing. It was a revelation to me: I was delighted! Judge of my joy when on coming to Gilcomston in 1945 and learning that the temporary organist, Verden Sykes (who had a similar extemporary gift to that of Gordon, but not the same biblical knowledge) would not accept the post as a permanency, the advertisement in the newspaper brought a response from Gordon Ross.

Gordon had begun to attend our mid-week Bible Studies which were started within weeks of my arrival; so I said to the Committee, I would have no one else but Gordon Ross. This was a little awkward for myself, because the son of the organist at St. Paul's Church where I had ministered for six months during a vacancy had offered himself for the post also and we had been good friends. It was not easy to say no, but I knew whom I wanted, and thirty-nine years of Gordon Ross' playing and our close fellowship together in the praise of our Lord - to say nothing of his power as an intercessor in our prayer meetings - has done nothing to cause me to regret that determination. It was of God, as many thousands now all over the world and many in Glory would agree.

The loss of Gordon Ross when the Lord took him home was a great blow, and I wondered whether the work would ever recover. Drew Tulloch who came as a pupil of Merle Ingram's from Shetland years before and joined our congregation was now a music teacher in local schools and a concert pianist. He was willing to play in the interim, but regarded himself primarily as a pianist not an organist. And beside, could he work with me and please me?

Well, first of all, he was an accomplished musician and was able to read and play work that would have taxed our brother, Gordon, who was a natural more than a professionally trained musician - all the more credit to him for the rich spontaneity of his gift!

But Drew was a musician in the classical mould. How would he fit in to Gordon Ross's Gilcomston - or William Still's for that matter!? That was perhaps more his thought than ours, because there being no Gordon Ross around, and the only other prospect would be to seek a professional musician who might not have the same sympathy with our congregation and its ministry as Gordon and Drew both had, there was no alternative.

Drew was our man, and we would have to convince him that he was, and ask the Lord to confirm it to him. The Lord must have done so, for in the end Drew agreed, and the result has been an increasingly enriching experience of his sensitive and intelligent playing, with a great respect for words as well as music, and with a flare for finding music with allusions to the Word of God and to the hymns chosen.

A word ought to be said about another Andrew, Bruce by surname, the son of a Motherwell minister, who came to Aberdeen to study music and is now a teacher at the local Grammar School. These two Andrews are great friends, and Andrew Bruce is virtually assistant organist at Gilcomston at the present time, and his fine playing is deeply appreciated. How wonderful to have such Christians leading our praise!

I can hardly realise my good fortune in that the Lord in his extreme generosity has provided once again an organist and an assistant in complete sympathy and harmony with the work, and with whom it is sheer pleasure to work. Surely goodness and mercy have followed us even to this present day!

To hear the volume of the congregation's singing and to sense their intelligent commitment to the high privilege of praising God is something for which I think I am undyingly grateful. Laudate Dominum!

CHAPTER 16

WORK WITH CHILDREN

Apart from having been a child, and having been brought up in the midst of a family of six, one destined like myself to remain a bachelor had little qualification for working with children - beyond a love of them (I dread taking fragile infants in my arms, even for baptisms! 'Father,' I cry, 'you hold the little one!').

I had little to do specifically with children's work until I became organist of the Gallowgate Church and had a keen children's choir. While a student I also worked with children in choirs and increasingly in dramatic presentations, such as 'In a Persian Market' which I have described. These times are full of happy memories for me and some of these youngsters of long ago are still in touch with me today.

I had little to do with children during my assistantship at Springburnhill, Glasgow, but arriving at Gilcomston in the summer of 1945, found a Sunday School so run down that something had to be done. The suggestion was made that we hold a Children's Church at 3 p.m. on Sunday afternoons and invite all children but the Infants and Primary. We soon had as many as seventy children, and because our new organist, Gordon Ross was willing to become one of our teachers, we used the Church and the organ, and soon had a children's choir of perhaps thirty children. They sang a piece each Sunday until singing developed into dramatic presentations of Bible

stories when many stirring afternoons were held with Gordon
at the organ supplying background music to a whole series of
biblical dramas: the stoning of Stephen with paper stones, the
use of ancient pewter vessels for Belshazzar's feast; we even
had our children strung round the church and up and over the
pulpit steps to illustrate the number of generations between
Sarah and our Lord's mother, Mary. All sorts of things took
place, with a rehearsal every Wednesday evening at 6.30
before mid-week Bible Study. These children enjoyed the
free run of the premises and many are the memorable experiences these erstwhile youngsters still love to recall. They
say, 'Do you remember the day we did so and so...?''

I cannot recall nor find in the records how long Children's
Church continued on Sunday afternoons, but it would have
been after twelve years of coping with three major involve-
ments each Sunday - morning, afternoon, and a long evening
session - that I was relieved of the children's work when John
Smith, a born teacher undertook it at the changed time of after
the morning service. Others also involved in Sunday School
beyond the Children's Church stage were William Leslie,
George Sinton and Alan Masson all of whom did excellent
work until the whole question of the tension between Church
services and the teaching of the young was brought into the
melting pot. I should say that the Primary and Beginners
Sunday School has continued uninterrupted throughout the
entire ministry, in turn under Margaret Petrie, Aileen Stewart, Helen Smith, Eleanor Leslie, Agnes Lyall and Myrtle
Stephen.

The reason for raising the question of the teaching and
training of the young was the fact that we were still losing our
young people after Sunday School years although young
peoples' meetings of various kinds were tried. Even the
children of devoted members seemed to fade away from early

teenage years and it became such a heartbreak that serious thought had to be given to it.

I owe it to David Searle who then as Minister of Newhills in our Presbytery with special responsibility for children's work did some research, and reminded us all that Sunday Schools were first started, not for the children of church members and officebearers, but for unchurched youngsters. The training of our own young people should be in the hands of the minister and godly parents.

This set me thinking deeply, and I came to the conclusion (and many have since said the same), that Sunday Schools (apart from the fact that teachers became younger and younger and less and less experienced and Sunday Schools were often regarded as the 'Cinderella' of church activities) as well as other uniformed youth organisations were simply keeping youngsters from Church and from becoming involved in Church life from early teens onwards. There was a shocking wastage. What were we to do about it?

I conceived the idea of ceasing all Sunday Schools after beginners and Primary age (seven years) and invited parents to have their children sit with them in the family pew from the age of eight. This was considered not only revolutionary but bad, since little ones of that age would not sit so long, and even if they did, how much would they take in? I was determined to try it, and gained the co-operation from most of our officebearers, although some had qualms.

It was a costly change. Several parents objected and one family left our congregation over it. But the aim was simply to get children from the intelligent age of eight to sit in church and become accustomed to doing so. Thus at the age of their usual departure, when children considered themselves too old for Sunday School and when even youth meetings did not bring them to church, they would have formed the habit of being in church with their parents. There would be no awkward transition at the difficult adolescent age. It took several years to see if this worked, but in the end it did wonderfully, and the problem of losing children at thirteen and fourteen was definitely solved.

Of course, youngsters of eight and over did not understand all that took place in Church, but it was suggested that they might be allowed to sit and work with pencil and paper or even have interesting literature to look at as long as they did not disturb the service. Several parents tried this, and some sat in the gallery where their fidgets were less noticeable and one can only commend the co-operation of many parents in this experiment.

However, in time the aids to engage the interest of these children gradually disappeared, and in one case they did so because on discussing at home during lunch what the minister had said during the sermon, more than once a little voice piped up and said, 'That's not what the minister said!' Ah! pencils and paper and childish magazines notwithstanding, the children were listening.

This didn't entirely surprise me, because at a later stage, following the re-assessment of the work at the end of 1965 when according to the records, 'the result of the new quickening was that the whole ministry had to be tightened up'; we now 'began to be concerned that our children and younger folk might attend the services, morning and evening which were now more tolerable and interesting'. So we started children's addresses. There had been none of these during the first twenty years of the ministry, which seems to me now, amazing!

Yet, such has been the disastrous dispersion of congregations by the common practice of segregating the church family into every conceivable category of division of ages, sexes, etc., that for all these years children were almost anywhere but in church with their parents or guardians. And yet, it was from little children, mostly by question and answer, that I learned how much from the age of three to seven they could remember, understand and bring forth from their training in our excellent Primary Sunday School and from parents' teaching at home. 'Out of the mouths of babes and sucklings' I have heard some of the most amazing answers, even causing the congregation to gasp!

All the modern twaddle about little children not being able to understand profound and even abstract things was proved to be largely groundless, and a great deal of modern educational theory was seen to lead simply to a weakening of intellectual content in the teaching of children and had to be abandoned in face of the ability of youngsters to understand and think and provide devastating answers to simple and not so simple questions.

Surely the testimony of over one thousand children's addresses of which some are already published* bears out the assertion that little children can understand far more than secular professional educationists may believe or understand. Most of these were given to three to seven year olds, but also during summer holidays they were aimed at a slightly higher age group.

Certainly one of the most intriguing, engaging and fascinating aspects of the ministry has been on a Sunday morning to sit down as near these precious little ones as enabled one to see their eyes, and for a brief five minutes in the midst of a service which otherwise made no concession to them, to seek to bring out the truth of the lesson about to be unfolded to the grown-ups, that both the little ones would get something out

* William Still *Talks To The Children* published by Christian Focus Publications 1990

of it, and the grown-ups would receive the kernel of the main lesson about to be tackled in the sermon. The integration of these two parts of the service have thus provided a wonderful incentive to choose praise which would support and illuminate the lesson, thus making the service an entity. I would like to think that most aspects of Christian doctrine have been presented to these children over the years, and this has to some extent been confirmed by the collections of these addresses made by Aileen Stewart under thematic headings.

The truth is that since we abandoned Sunday Schools for children beyond the age of seven years, we have scarcely lost a young person at the transitional adolescent years. Indeed most of them have been taking communion (with the specific approval of the minister and their parents) from the age of seven or eight, and most of them profess faith in early or middle teen years and soon after ask to be placed on the congregational roll as full members. This had various advantages: one in particular is the growing integration of the congregation as a family of all ages in one unsegregated fellowship.

* * * * * *

The other aspect of work among the young which has vitally interested me is that of Infant Baptism. Baptism is always a vexed subject, especially where there are inter-denominational contacts. But it was not until the late 1950s that the subject was brought forcefully to my mind by couples about to become parents, who wanted to know what was taking place and what they were supposed to know and believe and do.

Earlier I had an unusual experience associated with this call from parents to baptise a child. It was the case of Arthur Farman for whom his parents wished baptism as the child was very sick. Indeed little Arthur Farman was dying of Pink Disease. I was very wary that the request may have been made out of superstition - he could not die without the baptismal blessing or some such thing. But having explained that there was no necessity for baptism before he died, I agreed to do so.

As I prayed over the child I sought God's will for this child, 'Lord,' I said, 'You could save this bairn if you wanted.' And that is just what he did! To the surprise of the doctors Arthur made a full recovery and every year since I have had some form of contact with his grateful parents. Years afterwards I had the pleasure of greeting Arthur after a Christmas service as he stood resplendent in his naval uniform and it had been my delight in more recent years to officiate at his wedding.

This was not the first time that this has happened. I had a similar experience when I was asked to baptise another infant who had been pronounced dying. As with the Farmans I underlined that this could not be a superstitious ritual before taking the child and praying over it. Again I prayed saying that God could recover this child if it was his will and that we were asking him to do so. I have lost trace of the young girl now who must be quite grown up. Her people were from Banchory and for years grateful contact was made.

I do not know if it was because of these instances or because something more general was supposed to be discerned in me, but it was powerfully suggested that I had a healing gift and I was urged to make use of it. I was doubtful of the auspices which seemed to me to be too spirit conditioned, and as I thought of the sensation which could arise around the church if a whole lot of worldly people should seek healing for their bodies without healing for their souls, I adamantly refused. It should be emphasised, however, that I believe many have been healed through the quiet believing prayers of our inter-cessors. Indeed some of our most prominent members and officebearers would be the first to acknowledge that they believe they owe their survival, largely, if not entirely, to the prayers of the Lord's people. The lesson surely is, quietly does it!

The growing questions concerning baptism, however, drove me to study the doctrine of Covenant Baptism in detail and with fullness: first, that I myself might be sure where I stood, and then that I would be able with confidence to assure young believing parents as to what was involved for them.

For a comparison of God's Covenant with Abraham in respect of circumcision in Genesis 17 (with Paul bringing circumcision and Baptism together as meaning the same in Colossians 2:11,12) it became clear that Christian Baptism of the infants of believers was an act of faith in which parents and the whole Church were involved. It is a promise to bring the little one up in the faith by prayer, precept and example; and particularly is an act of faith which is a challenge to receive the gift of faith for the child's salvation as for one's own.

This has had wide repercussions and much has been spoken and written on the subject. However, 'the proof of the pudding is in the eating': over thirty years I have had opportunity to see how effectual such 'claiming' faith can be. The results, as far as our congregation is concerned have amply justified this stand upon the biblical verities of Covenant Baptism. I have seen parents believe and hold on to faith for their children even when in early teen years they have wriggled and even rebelled, and they have seen them come through not only to convinced, but to active faith and service of Christ in his church.

There was one example of a widowed mother who wrung her hands when her only daughter of about thirteen years stamped her foot and said she was not a Christian and was not going to be a Christian! What was the believing mother to do?

Tell her she can do nothing about it, since that was decided for her long ago. It worked, and that young girl, herself a mother today in a far-away land is serving the Lord faithfully with her Christian husband and bringing up their little boys in the same assured faith.

Of course, there is nothing automatic about such a proceeding, as the presumed circumcision of Esau and Jacob prove. This is where the mystery of election comes in: it is impossible to believe that Isaac and Rebekah had faith for Esau's salvation, since we know (Hebrews 12:16) that he is in hell. Certainly Rebekah was given an intimation about the twins before their birth, but that prediction seemed to concern service rather than destiny. The mystery of election entered into their situation, as indeed it must enter into ours. All that believing parents can do is to obey God's covenant command in a spirit of absolute surrender to the will of God, even being prepared to die a death to self for the sake of the salvation of their children (see Col. 1:24); then bringing them up believingly as little Christians from the earliest age, with the confident assurance that they are the Lord's - if one can come through to that assurance by the gift of faith.

CHAPTER 17

A BACHELOR MINISTER

I suppose it is not unnatural for those interested in the life of a minister to enquire what difference it makes being a bachelor. It is not an easy subject to discuss, especially if the apostle Paul's stance were taken in 1 Corinthians 7:7, where he says, 'I would that all men were even as myself'. However, he immediately qualifies that by saying, 'But every man has his proper gift of God, one after this manner and another after that'; so that he was not really proposing the abolition of the human race!

A more spacious aspect is that of our Lord in Matthew 19:3-12 in answer to the Pharisees' question about divorce and their suggestion that because of the difficulties associated with marriage, it was better not to marry. Jesus disagreed, although he admitted that not every one could accept the teaching of Genesis 2:24 to which he had just referred . He adds, 'For some are eunuchs because they were born that way; others were made that way by men; and others have renounced marriage because of the kingdom of heaven. The one who can accept this should accept it.'

So marriage although it is God-ordained and natural, is not for everyone. Jesus' third category is interesting - those who have renounced marriage because of the kingdom of heaven. That has always seemed to me so noble that not many men would admit to such sacrifice. I suspect that with most

Christian men who could have married and haven't including ministers, it was more a matter of divine appointment, even for some, alas, disappointment, rather than quixotic renunciation.

It is true that from the age of sixteen or so an inner conviction possessed me that I would never marry. That went against the grain of a romantic nature but, despite the dread of loneliness and unfulfilment, so it has proved. It was the Holy Spirit who intimated to me, a sensitive creature by any standards, that a life of singleness, celibacy, with all its unutterable personal loneliness was to be mine. I couldn't have been surer of anything in life than I could about that intimation. There was no sudden vision or anything of that kind but the Lord just came and made it perfectly clear. That was part of my consecration, but the thought of a whole life stretching out at ghastly length was overpowering: the infinity of a life that was to be lived on my own and in a sense with no one but Jesus Christ, and I didn't know Jesus Christ well enough then to think how wonderful that would be.

How often I sat at the keys of my piano, the grand piano my father gave me because he thought the only thing in the world that I was interested in was music (he didn't know the other things that were in my heart until later in life), sitting there longing for fellowship, companionship, friendship and the utter agony of that experience to a largely unformed personality at the age of seventeen or so. We older people must never forget this with regard to young people, that their suffering can be something just about as hellish as the human soul can endure. Certainly it seemed to me then, and I try to recall it when youngsters come to me with their hearts broken. On reflection it still seems to me that there is something hellish about it. Perhaps that is why one so readily relates to naughty and anguished young people. The tears that I shed at that piano

vainly searching for chords, fumbling over the keys - talk
about the Lost Chord! - chords that would express my agony,
my anguish. I think of some of these chords now, that I have
subsequently found in people like Wagner and Tchaikovsky,
Sibelius, Delius, Rimsky-Korsakov, and others later than
these. I suppose one has to get it out in some sort of expression.
Others would find another medium of expression than the
piano, or music: painting or something, even violence. But
even expressing it, this frustration, this blockage of one's way
towards what in one's innocence and ignorance one regards
as legitimate fulfilment, is not solved even in the case of, say,
Beethoven. Think of the agonising occasions when he used
his immortal music to bless and delight others. Many thousands, even millions, have been blessed by the sweetness and
glory of his music but even when it was finished, for him that
did not solve his agony; not at all. It did not solve any problem.

Yet for all this tortured frustration it would be wrong for
me not to underline what the advantages of the Lord's
appointment for me have been, the disadvantages being
obvious. I remember one occasion when I spoke at the
Palmerston Place convention in Edinburgh with Stanley
Voke, then of Sunderland. We had had tea together in the
afternoon and I was telling him that I was a bachelor. That
night while he was in the pulpit and I was sitting down in the
choir stalls having given my address, Stanley, who was
preaching on Ephesians, suddenly decided to use me as a
focus for his sermon. Turning towards me in front of the
whole congregation he said, 'A man is only half a man until
he is married!' I was shocked and suddenly felt cold and hot
all at once as if everyone was looking at me. Then as I sat and
pondered the unkindness of that cut, I thought this, and it has
been a comfort to me ever since: 'Poor Jesus!'

I can honestly say now that I am glad the Lord did not

provide a wife for me, because the advantages have far outweighed the disadvantages. True, some people would think that a woman in a manse was essential, and doubtless most married ministers would think it inconceivable that they could have carried out their ministry without their helpmeet.

I perfectly understand that point of view, and from my knowledge of many manse families, having been in at the beginning of many of them through conducting their marriages, I rejoice at the wonderful partnership of many, and have been blessed by many, too!

However, the great advantage of celibacy in the ministry has been the degree of freedom one has enjoyed. Often it has been possible to reduce home considerations, consonant with care for one's health and well-being, to the minimum which is not possible where there is a wife and possibly children for whom one is responsible, if one has contracted to marry and beget children.

Of course in my case the freedom has not been altogether absolute for being far from domesticated but fortunately spending the most of my life in my home town, I have had the support of my family.

Where there has been need in my ministry for a feminine hand, and that has been often, especially among our own congregation, I have found that there has always been a motherly soul to whom one could refer persons in need of that kind of care or counsel. And, of course in dealing with womankind, any minister has to be careful about interviews and consultations. It is not always good to interview a woman alone, and one has occasionally had to enlist the help of another man or woman to be present.

* * * * * *

In the first five years of ministry, Auntie was always on hand to fulfil these duties. Indeed it was certainly not just the ladies of the congregation who sought her counsel but many men as well, including myself.

My Aunt was a true helpmeet to me. She had a very tender heart and endeared herself to many of the old Gilcomston folk who found the new evangelistic ministry hard to take. I'm sure she did more for me in that regard that I knew. I can recall on one occasion after fierce resistance to the Gospel I had at last come round to the doctrine of hell and judgment for those who refuse and resist the invitation to come to Christ. She gently remonstrated with me.

It had happened that for about three months, whatever the subject, in the end I had came round to the dire prospect of a Christless eternity. I knew it was getting people down, and yet, at that time it was such a burden on my heart that I could do nothing but discharge it on their hapless heads. I had preached the Gospel to them in every way but they would not have it. They said, 'This is the Salvation Army, not the Church of Scotland.' I showed them from Scottish history and the Bible that long before the Salvation Army or William Booth, this was the truth of God, but they wriggled and turned until in the end what could I do? I said, 'If you will not have the Gospel from God's Holy Book and from his servant anointed to come here and give it to you, then this is the alternative.'

After that, whatever the subject, like Noah's dove three times round the ark and home, we gravitated to the subject of hell. Of course every topic in the Bible is related to hell and heaven somehow or another, isn't it? I never did the like again, but I am sure that by it I smashed an opposition to the Gospel by douce Kirk folk and I believe it was necessary to the establishment of the work. Even now with many regrets about the early years of the ministry, I cannot regret that teaching even if others who remember it cringe at the memory, since I knew, that it, if anything was of the Lord.

Yet I remember so well one Sunday at lunch time when the Word had been particularly hard and hell had been our topic for weeks, in discussion my Aunt spoke out. 'I am sitting there with them in the pew and taking it all,' she said. 'I feel for them. Oh, Willie,' she cried, 'is there no love in the Gospel?' That shook me, and yet I had to say, 'I can do nothing but what the Lord has laid on my heart.' 'Well', said Auntie, 'if it goes on, there will soon be no one there but you and me!' 'And will you desert me, then?' I asked. 'Never,' she said, with conviction: 'I committed myself to you and the Lord's work here and I will never leave you.' And there were happier days after that.

* * * * * *

Of course there was need for domestic help in the manse, and since my friendship with Mrs. Marjory Sinton which had begun in my student days had continued because she began to attend Gilcomston, the natural thing was to ask her to help my Aunt to look after the manse. Thus began one of the finest friendships I have ever seen. These two were like sisters, and shared many deep things, not least about the welfare of Mrs. Sinton's three practically fatherless boys. And although my Aunt's passing when she was suddenly stricken with cerebral haemorrhage and never regained consciousness was the greatest blow of my life, I am sure that it was an equal blow to Mrs. Sinton. That was in January, 1950. Still, forty years on, there is a far-away look in Mrs. Sinton's eyes when I mention Auntie.

This sudden loss when the work was beginning to deepen and things were somewhat smoother at the Church threw into the melting pot what my subsequent lifestyle was to be. It has been interesting to me to see how other bachelor ministers have solved this problem, some more easily than others because of their domestic gifts, especially in cooking. Who was to be my housekeeper? My cousin, Evelyn West (now Mrs. Peter Snelson) was living with us at the manse at the time, having graduated and become a school teacher and she remained to help for a time. But that wasn't fair on her and when her sister Rosemary came to Aberdeen to train as a nurse, they wanted to be together. What was I to do? I didn't want a stranger in the manse, however efficient, and this is perhaps part of what the good Lord knew which I didn't then, that I was a bit of a loner, and although I could feel desperately lonely, as any one can when under the weather or discouraged, I felt I needed my home to myself, to enable me to devote my time completely without distraction to the work.

Mrs. Sinton would do all she could, but she had three sons to care for and could only give so many hours in the day to attend to the manse. I therefore naturally turned to the family and to my father, mother and eldest sister, Barbara, and they were wonderful. It was arranged that I would have my main meal at midday with them, and this largely solved the problem.

That arrangement has obtained for forty years, encompassing my father's death in 1960 and my mother's death in 1967. My dear eldest sister Barbara has had the responsibility of attending to practically all my creature comforts ever since, and still does although at the time of writing she is in her eighty sixth year.

During those forty six years there has been, of course a succession of excellent helpers at the manse to whom I have owed a very great deal. After Mrs. Sinton, there was Mrs. Low whom I had known from my Salvation Army days; Mrs. Smith, a dear widow lady whom I still visit occasionally in hospital; there was Mrs. Fettes who helped most devotedly until her husband passed away; and one of the best has been

Mrs. Vera Hardie who came to Gilcomston in the early days
of the ministry from John Knox Church, Mounthooly where
I had been student assistant. No man could be more indebted
to womankind than I, and I retain the deepest respect for
women, not least from what I see of their part in the Lord's
work from biblical times to the present day. More recently
Mrs. Wymess has come to help me, another gain!

Another area of great help has been the secretaries I have
had. In the earliest days of 1945 and '46 when the work of
correspondence became overwhelming, not least in connection with away engagements coming in thick and fast following our first sensational days, a neighbour of my friend, James
Philip, Ian Geddes by name was looking for such work and
came to help. He was an excellent fellow, fully in sympathy
with the work, and he had the advantage of a car licence before
I had. Since my father generously gifted me an Austin 8 in
gratitude for what Gilcomston came to mean to him, Ian drove
me around even to meetings north and south, as indeed others
did at times, such as James Philip and John Breeze.

The next secretary was Rosemary Adams, who after the
deeply lamented death of her husband, Stanley, my dear
friend became part-time Secretary to Dr. David Short the
heart specialist and then part-time with me. Rosemary and I
who had collaborated for years in choice of pieces for her to
sing, especially at the Christmas Eve midnight service, was
with me for years and was a great help since she was
accustomed to the use of a dictaphone, which meant that
letters dictated early morning were ready for her to type when
she arrived.

However, Rosemary was all the time training for higher
service, as her daughter Shona grew up. Eventually she was
fortunate to gain a post with the Commercial College as a
lecturer. About that time my friend from student days, Edith

Ingram was being advised to seek lighter work than that of Secretary to the Mathematics Department of the University. Edith was ready to step into the breach, and was with me for eighteen years and more until it was time for her to rest. I cannot say what these many years of close companionship with Edith meant to me in the work. It was invaluable to have one so confidential, devoted and friendly to share the burdens of the work. I have a drawer absolutely packed with her shorthand notebooks, and the volume of letters there must be phenomenal!

It was a great sorrow to me when the onset of Edith's present infirmity made it hard and then impossible for her to continue at the manse. Indeed she went on much longer than was good for her, because of her complete commitment to the work. My gratitude to her for these many years of faithful support in so many ways could never be expressed in words. It is a great joy that Edith is still able to attend worship and prayer and Bible Study, which is really life to her.

What was I to do now? The Lord was preparing another helper. For years I had been concerned about Audrey Strichen's welfare, especially after the death of her dear companion, Margaret. When she was suddenly made redundant by the Voluntary Service, she was the obvious choice, and so now Audrey with her valuable experience of various kinds of office work including business experience has been a great help, and has been unfailing in her kind support of the work at the manse - apart from a great deal of private service she gives to the needy.

Of course, beyond and behind all this has been perhaps the most indefatigable worker of Gilcomston, my friend of many years, May Tough, whose family had had Salvation Army connections when I was a boy. May came to work in my father's fish merchant's office, and although an Anglican devoted to the worship of St. Margaret's, Gallowgate, she began to come to Gilcomston, and eventually joined. May loved to type, and type she did for all these years, especially after Lexie Thomson became so engrossed in University service that she was unable to continue her expert work.

It was mainly Congregational Records that May typed, and then books and booklets, despite her arduous service with the Health Board. After retirement May devoted herself the more to the work, and when Edith Ingram became less able for the demanding task of typing correspondence, May undertook that also by means of dictating cassettes.

During the last years of May's life, with her super word processor she kept a record of all the letters typed and from time to time would tell that they numbered hundreds. The liaison between May and Alan Masson, our chief printer who has been with us for more than thirty years, and myself worked wonderfully well, and with the help of John Linn, the computer expert and others, the work of much printing has gone on through the years. The death of May Tough after an amazingly short illness was a great blow to us all, and after many months we at Gilcomston have not yet recovered. In addition to all her work for Gilcomston and much typing of theses besides, May practically ran the Scripture Union book shop and supervised the voluntary workers. All this work had to be parcelled out to others, and despite our great loss it is marvellous today to think that so much of that work has been delegated to other willing workers.

As far as manse correspondence is concerned, although Audrey Strichen did not profess to be a typist, with a typewriter installed in her home she has helped that work greatly, but with my own word processor I have found it possible to do a good deal of that work myself.

* * * * * *

There are many other indefatigable workers to whom I am
deeply indebted; and although it is dangerously invidious to
mention names amongst so many, I must mention several.
One is our Session Clerk of so many years, William Leslie.
What the work owes to him is quite incalculable. For one
thing, that he has survived so many decades the onset and
development of his physical trouble and still to be around
despite much surgery and great suffering is a miracle of God's
grace and power. For a long time we felt that our brother's life
hung on a thread, but the latest surgery seems to have
recovered him wonderfully, and it is our great joy to have him
in the midst watching over so many things, extending the
wonderful hospitality of his home with Eleanor to so many
and sharing the conduct of our services in giving the intima-
tions.

Another whose service has been very special is Aileen
Stewart who has been with us since the very earliest days. One
of Aileen's principal gifts has been editorial. Very little has
passed through our own printing press as well as that of others
which has not undergone her expert scrutiny. To have had one
with such judgment and discretion to help with the demands
for so many words, words, words from so many directions has
made Aileen's task beyond all praise.

Then there is our Church Officer of over forty years, James
Sinton. I must tell a story about dear James. Because of bitter
experience in youth, James for a time became disillusioned
with religion, but his mother enlisted the prayers of my Aunt,
Mrs. Alexander. In the fullness of time when the Sinton
family became increasingly integrated with Gilcomston, James
began to attend. It so happened that he was attending one
Sunday morning when there was communion at the close of
the service. However, that was the terrible morning when my
Aunt lay unconscious from a cerebral haemorrhage in the

infirmary and never regained consciousness, so that she never knew on earth that her prayers were so abundantly answered in that James took communion that morning. Later, when there was need of a Church Officer, it was made perfectly clear to him that the Lord was calling him to this office. It has not always been easy for James, but God has enabled him to keep at it all these years, and even although he has been retired from work for many months now, he is still active, and we are undyingly grateful to him for all his service.

James Shearer has been our Treasurer since Walker Leith gave it up many years ago, and we owe more to James' skilful keeping of our finances than we could ever say. His has been a major task, and his pleasantness in helping us and all good causes that need material support is one of the delightful features of our fellowship.

I must also mention three other men; one is dear John Hardie who has been almost all these years a faithful member and officebearer of Gilcomston and a dear friend. John has served as Clerk to our deacons as well as in the YMCA; and beyond his great gift for friendship, he has a deep burden for missionary work and is a most faithful intercessor. He and dear Vera whom I've known since 1943 at John Knox Mounthooly are amongst the most treasured of our fellowship.

The other two happen to be first cousins: Frank Lyall, Professor of Public Law in Aberdeen University, who is our Clerk to the Deacons' Court, and who has been invaluable with his expert knowledge of the law and of procedures of many kinds; and Ramsay Robb has looked after our buildings for many years since the demise of John Fordyce, and not least in the negotiations concerning the necessary truncation of our spire. Along with the knowledgeable help of Albert Rodger who is involved with the Property Committee of Presbytery, he has been untiring in looking after the interests of the buildings in which God has blest so many over many years - and is still blessing!

* * * * * *

These pages were intended to be about a bachelor minister! Perhaps the extraordinary devotion of so many people recorded here (and there are many more, which is bound to make it invidious to mention any and not others) is some indication of how it has been possible for a man, seemingly on his own, but supported by armies of committed helpers, to keep going so long.

EPILOGUE

80TH BIRTHDAY

Looking back on certain landmarks of my career, I would say that the transition from evangelisticism to systematic exposition of the Scriptures in January 1947 was probably the most significantly decisive moment of my life.

After that I can think of nothing so significant, although plenty events had been recorded here, until my return from holiday in Israel when the Lord intimated to me that I was to remain at Gilcomston even though I had been here already for twenty years.

Beyond that there was nothing remarkable until my seventieth birthday in 1981 when a good deal was made of the occasion with presentations and a musical evening in the church, I and others taking part. That should really have been my musical swansong if the playing mistakes as recorded on tape are anything to go by! But the 'swan' refuses to 'die', so up he comes again, as determined as ever to play at his eightieth!

On my seventy-fifth birthday a Festschrift was presented to me to which my academic friends had contributed. That was in St. George's Tron, Glasgow when I was asked to give a Rutherford house address. *What of the future?* was the title I chose. From a personal point of view, I felt then as I feel now, that I am in more excellent health than I have ever been and I'll go as long as I am enabled.

191

I said to our esteemed Session Clerk, William Leslie after the seventy-fifth celebration, 'Now, no more celebrations!' 'No,' he said, 'not until your eightieth!' Little did I think...

I wanted it to be as modest as possible, not to grieve the Lord but from 'a little music, not much to say and a cup of tea', it grew until we had a Kirk full of people from all over, and a very blessed evening which I think gave glory to God.

I had said that anyone who wanted to mark the occasion could contribute to the organ fund - which will be our next expense after we spend a million and a half restoring our buildings! - and well over £4000 was given. I was grateful and glad to help towards the renewing of the instrument which, handled so well, has inspired our praise for so long.

They speak light-heartedly of my ninetieth but that is in higher hands. I will be content to labour on as long as he gives me strength. What a relief not to have to decide things like that - or anything else. He does it all - bless HIM!